The Alpine Game

An amateur climber's quest for the 4000m peaks.

By Nick Kelso

Illustrations by James Hunt

Copyright © *2007* **Nick Kelso**

All rights reserved by the author. No part of this publication may be reproduced, stored in a retrieval system or transmitted in any form or by any means electronic, mechanical, photocopying, recording or otherwise, without the prior written permission of the author.

First published December 2007.

To Michael, Katie, Rhiannon, Eleanor and Jack.
May they find their own games to play.

About the author

Nick Kelso was born in Nigeria in 1962, and spent his childhood in both the UK, and the Netherlands. He was educated at Brockenhurst College and Lancaster University where he read Philosophy and History. He is author of Errors of Judgement, (Hale 1988), and currently works for Philips, promoting energy efficient lighting. In 2000 he emigrated to the Netherlands, where he lives with his wife Agata and two children, Michael and Katie.

Contents

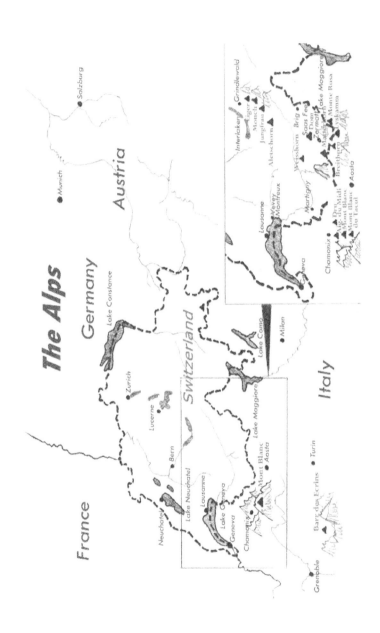

Illustrations

1. Eiger summit 1984
2. Eiger summit view 1984
3. Matterhorn team 1987
4. Mont Blanc 1988
5. Hornli Hut - Priest blessing 1989
6. Matterhorn summit 1989
7. Eiger - climbing buttresses 1990
8. Jeckyl bar celebrating with Tony 1990
9. North Wall Bar New Team ID 1994
10. Dolomites - JR abseils 1994
11. Castor - Jerry bivis en route 1994
12. Mönch team 1995
13. Signalkuppe summit shot 1996
14. Mer de Glace - James bivi 1996
15. Alpine start Monte Rosa 1996
16. Tour Ronde - James 1997
17. Zoe & Agata - Breithorn 1998
18. Allalinhorn summit 2000
19. Bishorn weekend 2001
20. Barre des Ecrins 2005
21. Agata & Katie - Chamonix 2002
22. Cosmique arête 2005
23. Dome des Neige summit 2005
24. Mer de Glace climate change 2007

Copyright - all photographs' Nicholas Kelso.
All sketches and drawings reproduced by kind permission of James Hunt.

Foreword

There are 82 Alpine 4000m peaks and climbing or 'collecting' them all has become a lifetime's challenge for many climbers today. This story, which takes place during the last quarter of a century, is my own attempt at realizing the dream. I am a very ordinary climber. At my best I could lead UK 5a* but mostly 4a or 4b. Today I find V. Diff awkward, but that is the whole point of this book. It is 4000m peak ticking from the perspective of the 'ordinary Joe', and not the elite climber who makes it all seem easy.

I love the Alps and climbing in these mountains has left me with great memories. I am inspired by the peaks themselves, the places, the people, the views and the history - in short by the whole experience. I can also add that I love life, have absolutely no desire to die and have always tried to keep the 'game' within an overall perspective of life. Recently however, I have begun to struggle with the morality of Alpinism, whilst being a son, father and husband. This dilemma is an important element in the later part of this story.

I have also been extremely lucky to have great friends to climb with. These are some of the finest people I have ever met and over the years we have formed deep bonds. Anyone embarking on an Alpine expedition is taking part in a dangerous activity and those who rope up together share this risk.

Alpinism has so much to offer today that it is easy to forget this was not always the perception. Not so long ago the entire region was clouded in mystery and thought to contain all kinds of horrors.

*For an overview of climbing grades, see the appendix

One of my favourite stories is how the Professor of Physics at Zurich university in the early 18th century devoted a chapter of his latest book to the detailed descriptions of Alpine dragons, one of which he even claimed to have seen in the flesh.

Today climbing in the Alps is a life enhancing experience for many, but this new perception may be just as fleeting as the era of the dragons, for it is conceivable that in a few centuries, and for different reasons, as few people will venture into these mountains as did before the 18th century.

We have already seen what climate change means for the Alps, with shrinking glaciers, loosening rock faces and collapsing seracs. The prevailing wisdom is that this is being caused primarily by a rise in carbon emissions. I believe that many of the solutions we need to reduce our energy consumption already exist today, such as energy efficient lighting. They simply need to be utilised.

The Alps are simply magnificent and we should do all we can to preserve them as a valuable and beautiful resource for all. 'Save the snow' should be on all our minds.

Nick Kelso, Eindhoven, April 2009

Part One

1. A new game

Alpinism was one of the great discoveries of my life. The sheer joy of life it has engendered over the years has left me grateful to be born in an age, when the economic means to pursue it became available to ordinary people.

People are drawn to Alpine climbing from all walks of life and from all parts of the world. Even in the Netherlands, a country where the highest hill is barely noticeable, there is a thriving mountaineering culture. It seems to fulfil a need, provide meaning, discipline and structure. History, sport, culture and geography all come together to create this unique activity, which allows you to test your own personal limits and set your own goals. Its dangers, and there are many, are all part of the attraction.

Anyone who climbs in the Alps has started somewhere. It might be with parents, friends, or a local club or university association, but somehow a connection is made and the game begins. My own learning curve involved 'finding out the hard way', which is no bad thing, as long as you survive long enough for the lessons to be absorbed.

It all began for me in November 1983, when as an undergraduate, in my final year at Lancaster University, I watched a BBC programme about the North Face of the Eiger. This dramatically re-enacted some of the key moments during the early attempts to climb the face and really caught my imagination. This, in turn, led me to a book, well known in climbing circles, called 'The White Spider', a history of the early climbs on the Eiger North Face by the Austrian explorer Heinrich Harrer, who was himself in the first party to climb the face.

Eight out of the first ten climbers to attempt the route had died on it, and the subsequent story portrayed the climb as something approaching a definition of manhood. Sometimes in life a book leaves a lasting impression. 'The White Spider' had a dramatic impact on me and as a direct result I determined to climb the Eiger.

My preference was to find someone to climb it with but, if necessary, I would do it alone. By doing this I would become, so I reasoned, a small part of the mountain's history, but the real reason was the magnificence of the challenge. To climb this mountain, to achieve this goal would be to do something out of the ordinary. It would be more meaningful and inspiring than just starting work in a bank or something like it, and it also appealed to my passion for history and adventure.

My friends generally laughed and clearly doubted I was serious. A girlfriend pointed out some of the issues.

'Come on Nick, you've never climbed before, you don't have any equipment and you don't even know where the Eiger is.'

She was right on all counts, but to me this seemed to make the idea more worthwhile not less. The more people talked the idea down, the more determined I became. I would solve each of the problems in turn and develop a plan of action.

During the spring of 1984 I set about acquiring the basic knowledge and skills necessary. I went rock climbing with two friends, Rob Bracewell and John Carpenter, who taught me about rope work, route finding and belaying. We climbed in the quarries around Lancaster and also occasionally in the Lake District. At the time I spent a lot of time soloing easy routes - climbing without ropes or protection - in order to prepare for a possible solo ascent of the Eiger. In doing so I became aware of the climbing world, with all its rivalries, colourful characters and inspiring myths. It was a hard culture, particularly in Northern England, but to be involved even on the very fringe gave life an added depth.

Rob introduced me to some of his climbing friends from the CUMC (Cambridge University Mountaineering Club). We spent a week at Easter in 1984, rock climbing our way across the Lake District - moving from crag to crag, interspersed with evenings in some of the finest pubs in Britain. We were climbing or seconding up to about VS at this time.

I began to read widely, raiding the university library for anything on the subject of climbing. I also had long conversations with Rob who had already climbed in the Alps. He was still deeply troubled by two incidents. As a student at Cambridge one of his friends had been tragically killed near Chamonix, by a crevasse fall when descending the Dru – this was in 1983 I believe. He himself had survived a difficult and dangerous climb in the Vanoise, where he spent an hour descending an ice face knowing that a slip meant death. Rob had decided that 'the game' was not worth the candle, and had sworn not to go back to the Alps again, and certainly not with a novice, obsessed with another dangerous mountain.

However he was willing to do the next best thing and pass on his knowledge of Alpinism. So I learned of the need for early Alpine starts, the absolute need for speed, a good weather forecast and the kind of equipment I should take, for example an ice axe, crampons, helmet, good boots and a strong rucksack. I also began to hear some of the epic tales of climbing folklore - stories of survival against the odds and of great deeds done long ago. It was a strange new world, which completely fascinated me.

The question of which route I should try to climb on the Eiger took a little time to solve. Not that the North Face was an option. Even in my most optimistic moments I recognised this would be a step too far, but there were several ridges, which might have been possible. In the end, the choice of the West Face became obvious, - after I had bought a small blue Alpine guidebook edited by Robin Collomb. This listed the Eiger as a PD climb – Peu Difficile (Little difficulty) and also, encouragingly, as suitable for first time ascentionists. He did concede there was 'a threat from stone fall' but as PD was almost at the bottom of the list of grading difficulties I gained in confidence. 'How difficult can this be,' I thought. 'I'm already climbing harder than this on rock here.'

More inspiration was provided by the story of the first ascent of the Eiger in 1858 by Charles Barrington and his guides. He had no previous climbing experience either when he turned up as a young man in Grindelwald. After a guided ascent of the Jungfrau he had decided to have a go at the Eiger, on the basis that it had not yet been climbed. He had chosen the West Face, and although guided, he seems to have led the hardest parts of the climb himself and had reached the summit with a flag in hand. On the descent he was twice almost swept away by avalanches but made it back safely and in his own words *'seemed for the evening to be a 'lion.''*

I was also amused to learn that Queen Victoria had once asked her prime minister at the time, William Gladstone, about the possibilities of banning Alpine climbing on the basis that it was too dangerous and that many young aristocrats were dying. In a perverse way, the idea of doing something the old Queen disapproved of, only added to its attraction.

My fitness at the time was not an issue. I was playing football for hours on end, most days of the week and felt myself in the rude health of youth. I had always been good at sports, was not overweight and was confident my stamina would see me through the big day.

My psychological preparation on the other hand involved drinking beer. During the evenings, in the student bars around the campus, we developed a drinking game based on the Eiger. Eight key points of the 'Eigerwand' were identified and linked to pints of beer. So if you had drunk three pints you had passed the first ice field; five pints got you to death bivouac and eight pints meant the summit. However if you threw up after eight pints you were deemed to have fallen on the descent. The game linked two key interests. We loved beer, by which I mean real ale, for we were all CAMRA (Campaign for Real Ale) sympathisers and drank mainly 80 Shillings and Younger's No.3 although Boddingtons and Tetley's were also more than acceptable when available. A later variant of this game had us climbing Everest by drinking 70 pints in a week, but the less said about that the better.

During these bar sessions we talked, discussed and sometimes argued about the things that really mattered to us. The big issues of the time included Margaret Thatcher, Arthur Scargill and the miners' strike, apartheid in South Africa, nuclear deterrence and unemployment. We also discussed philosophy, but usually only during the first few pints after which our minds switched to talking about girls, football and other sports.

At the time I was reading for my degree in Philosophy and History. This included a special project on the Scottish Philosopher David Hume, for whom I had developed a deep sense of admiration and whose theory of knowledge and identification of the problem of induction fascinated me. I was also the President of the Lancaster University Parachute Club. Skydiving took up most of my weekends and I spent a good deal of time trying to persuade every girl I met to join me in this endeavour - not without success. These were idyllic days. Life was fun, stimulating and without real responsibility. We knew it was only a brief interlude before our working lives began and were determined to make it last as long as possible. Even now I look back on those days as being some of the best of my life.

Finals came and went, as did our graduation ceremonies. I got my 'Desmond' as expected and I remember lying in the sun on the grass, thinking about the rest of my life which at the time stretched out unimaginably far into the future. I was 22 and everything seemed exciting, full of promise, and possible. During the May Ball period a group of us went down to Cambridge and drank Pimms rather than beer. We successfully gate crashed the New Hall Ball, which did not require black tie, and which was where many of Cambridge's female students resided.

Back in Lancaster a number of us decided to stay on for the summer and rent a house. Sharon, Kath, Lucy, Rob, Paul and I all signed on the dole and enjoyed the fine summer weather whilst I now set about making the final preparations for my trip. I cycled a good deal during July around the valleys and hills of North West England and my alcohol intake diminished significantly as the impact of living on the dole was felt. With about three pounds to spend per day we grew adept at living on pulses for less than a pound. This left two pounds for beer, which in those days still meant three pints and a packet of crisps.

One thing however had not gone well. Despite many sales

pitches in recent months I hadn't managed to persuade anyone to join me on the climb and was now resigned to going alone. I decided to hitch hike to London and catch the boat train from there to Interlaken. This cost £76 return and left me with next to no money. My other purchase was a Joe Brown helmet for £25. I borrowed an ice axe and boots and used my old student rucksack. I also managed to scrounge an old tent, of the £20 summer-only variety, and a sleeping bag. This was pretty much it. At the last minute I threw in a copy of 'I Claudius' by Robert Graves. My departure date was set for 2nd August, and I would leave immediately after 'signing on'.

As time went by it dawned on a number of my friends that I was actually going to go through with the whole thing. Their concern became more evident and gentle attempts were made to dissuade me from going. Unbeknown to me, they were contemplating stealing my passport to prevent me from getting abroad. An even wilder idea, no doubt alcohol induced, had someone breaking my leg, but in the end they accepted the inevitable.

The big day finally came and I went to the local DHSS offices carrying a large rucksack from which a long ice axe was threatening to escape at any moment. But nobody in the queue seemed to care. Most of the people around me seemed to have the life crushed out of them and looked resigned and gloomy. My turn came: I yielded a quick signature and a cheque for £46, officially enough to keep me alive for another two weeks. The women behind the counter eyed me suspiciously but said nothing. Perhaps she thought my bike was outside. The whole process was fast and efficient, which was just as well, for at the time several million of my fellow countrymen were involved in the same sad process. Although Britain's economy was through the worst of the recession of the early 1980s, the employment situation in the North West remained poor.

After leaving the social security offices, I cashed my cheque and headed out for the hitch hiking post. This money was all I would have for the next two weeks so I had to be very cautious and spending it on travelling to London was clearly not an option. I arrived there by early evening, and met up with my two skydiving mates Tony O'Flaherty and Paul Taylor in a London pub. They were only vaguely aware of my plans and listened in growing disbelief.

'You're bloody mad, Kelso,' said Tony finally. 'I can't believe you're serious. What do you know about climbing?'

'Come on we used to do worse things parachuting.'

'No, we didn't. You're probably going to die.'

By now, however, I was fully used to and inured to these sentiments and just smiled. Nevertheless there was a forced cheerfulness about our conversations that evening and the beer tasted awful.

That night I stayed with Tony and his parents in South London and in the morning was given a lift to Waterloo station. My journey by train and boat to Interlaken more closely resembled that of the Victorian pioneers than I realised at the time. It certainly provided plenty of hours to think about the immediate future. I spent the time reading or just staring out of the window. Had I really gone too far ?, was I going to return in one piece ?, or the worst doubt of all, would I ever be found. There was one thing I was not bothered about: I had no climbing insurance. If I needed rescuing I would be in financial trouble but as I had no money, assets, or the immediate prospects of acquiring them, this did not unduly worry me.

The train to Zurich continued through the night. I remember talking to some English climbers in my carriage. They were going to Zermatt to climb the Matterhorn and I remember trying very hard not let on that I had never heard of the place, although I was well aware of the Matterhorn itself. They left the train at Zurich and for the last part of the journey I travelled alone.

My early morning arrival at Interlaken had an element of farce. The Eiger is still 20km from Interlaken and can be reached from two valleys, one heading up to Grindelwald, the other via Wengen. A mountain railway went via Wengen to my base camp, which was to be the Eiger Glacier station, and it was this I intended to take. However there was a catch. Wishing to save money I needed to walk the first part, to the third station along the route. This presupposed that I knew which way to go and on leaving Interlaken station I managed to walk for an hour in the wrong direction before realizing my error.

'Come on Kelso,' I thought. 'You've come here to climb the Eiger and you can't even navigate your way out of Interlaken.' For the first time being alone was an advantage!

I bought some food for the next few days, and then managed to get on the right track. Stopping briefly at Wengen, I was able to hire some crampons from a local climbing shop. Deciding to share my objective with the owner I showed him my guidebook. He traced the route for me, pretty much confirming what I already knew, but then finished by telling me to stay well away from the glacier on the right hand side of the face. Thus reassured, I arrived at the Eiger Glacier station just after midday.

To my surprise the weather was poor. It was August, and the middle of the summer, so it had not occurred to me that the skies would be anything other than sunny. New doubts arose. What if things didn't improve for a few days – would I have enough food and money to hold out? 'Probably not' was the answer.

In between the rain clouds I spotted signs of the West Face. It looked hard, cold and uninviting. Alongside were two more giants, the Mönch and the Jungfrau. My first task was to put up my fragile tent, on some ground below the station. It didn't exactly engender confidence, even before there was any wind, but I threw my equipment in and started to look around.

The Eiger Glacier station was a grim place. It consisted of a small waiting room, some toilets and a few storerooms. It may also have had a cafe bar but this was not open. It also seemed deserted which lent it a more disturbing aspect. Alongside was the Jungfrau railway track, which disappeared into a tunnel ahead of me. One of mankind's major wonders, this railway had been dug right through the Eiger and went on up to the Jungfraujoch. First completed in 1912, a further extension had been planned to the summit of the Jungfrau, which was fortunately shelved due to a lack of cash after the start of World War One. Now at regular intervals, trains passed which seemed almost exclusively filled with Japanese tourists. They all seemed to have cameras and for some reason even photographed me.

As evening approached I checked my food supplies. These

consisted of two tins of Ambrosia cream rice, a baguette with some sardines, a bag of wine gums and a couple of tins of Ravioli. All this I could and would eat cold. Water was available from the station toilets and I could read by the lights of the station. So with all the basics in place I turned in early that evening, full of excitement and expectation.

However that night a storm blew up and my worst fears about my tent were realized when, sometime after midnight the main pole buckled leaving me with a mass of flapping nylon above my head. There was only one thing to do. I evacuated my belongings and myself to the safety of the station toilets. These were quite roomy and allowed me to lie down and sleep flat out. I awoke before dawn to find a storm blowing and knew there would be no climbing that day.

I passed the hours by reading 'I Claudius', whilst lying on the platform in my sleeping bag. From time to time the trains would pass and again I smiled as the cameras flashed repeatedly. As time wore on the weather showed signs of improvement and towards evening two English climbers - also intent on climbing the Eiger, joined me. They were friendly and we chatted a bit, but it was clear neither party – if I could be considered a party - wanted to join forces the next day. We all retired early and this time sleep came more easily. I was up at 5.00am but the weather still seemed bad and another short sleep followed before I woke with a start at 8.00am to bright sunshine. This was much later than I had wanted to start, but I decided to take my chances. Within 20 minutes I was on my way, stopping briefly at the English guys' tent. They too had gone back to sleep after an early morning check, and I wanted to let them know that I 'was going for it.'

It took about 30 minutes of easy walking and scrambling to reach the first snowfield and I decided to climb straight up the rock buttresses ahead on the ridge. This was the route taken by Charles Barrington and his guides in 1858 during the first ascent of the West Face. He later described in a letter what had happened.

'So I went off about 300 or 400 yards over some smooth

rocks to the part which was almost perpendicular. I then waved the flag for them to come on, and after five minutes they followed and came up to me. They said it was impossible; I said, "I will try". So, with the rope coiled over my shoulders, I scrambled up, sticking like a cat to the rocks, which cut my fingers, and at last got up say 50 or 60 feet. I lowered the rope and the guides followed with its assistance.'

At the top of the first snow slope I came across my first ever Bergshrund and jumped across to a small ledge. From here it was all rock climbing at grade II and grade III. I made steady progress for a few hundred feet on a steep rock face until I reached the crux. This was a tricky move stepping across a blank bit of rock. Any fall now would be fatal, of that I was certain, and my doubts were amplified. What if it got harder still, I was almost certainly going to struggle to climb down what I had just come up.

I made the crux move hugging the rock closely and within a few minutes my confidence returned as the climbing eased considerably. It occurred to me vaguely as I looked back down the cliff I had just climbed, that I would need to find a different way down. However that was a problem for later, as for now I was fully committed to going up. I caught sight of the two English lads just starting up the snow slopes below. They had clearly decided to go for it too, and it was good to know I would not be the only person on the mountain. Ahead the steep cliffs stretched upwards and I stopped to consult my precious guidebook.

The route finding was tricky on this part of the climb, with the preferred line wending its way up gullies and moving around cliffs and other obstacles. Moving slowly upwards I managed to stay on route. About an hour later I was resting on a ledge overlooking the North Face when the English lads caught up with me. We chatted for a few minutes, exchanged photographs and they told me they had come up the first cliff by the guidebook route rather than my direct route.

For a while we climbed together un-roped, but they were stronger and within an hour they pulled away from me. The route involved a lot of scrambling and everywhere there was loose rock. In fact, most of the rocks on the face seemed to be loose and although there was nothing as hard as the first cliff, the face went on relentlessly. For hours I toiled upwards, past gullies and occasional snow slopes. At one stage I remembered my wine gums. One of the lessons I was to learn that day, and there were many, was that frozen wine gums are the last snack you need on a big mountain. It was impossible to chew them and I ended up swallowing a few of them whole.

It was mid-afternoon when I finally emerged onto the upper snow slopes. By now I was feeling rather tired, but the closeness of my goal kept me going, and above me I could see the English lads were near the summit. By now though my stops were becoming more frequent and the fine weather of the morning had been replaced by increasing cloud.

Just below the summit I came across hard ice for the first time. Moving clumsily I slipped and cut my knuckles badly although at the time it barely registered. I stopped to put on my crampons for the first time, and just after they were fixed the now descending English lads reached me. They were in good spirits.

'Watch out for the summit cornice - it's a really nasty one,' was their parting shot. It was to prove advice for which I would be grateful.

With my crampons on it took me another 20 minutes to the top and from here I could see along the summit ridge. It was snowy, but forewarned I approached with a caution I would not otherwise have felt. Suddenly I spotted the cornice overhanging the south face and shuddered at the thought of falling through it.

I had imagined this moment for months – sitting on the summit in the sun, eating drinking and enjoying the views. Now the reality was very different. I took off my rucksack and started taking photos. I had carried my hitchhiking board along too for some reason and now photographed this in the snow alongside my ice axe. I also managed to get some shots of the summit ridge of the Eiger and the Mönch, knowing these would be important proof.

Instinctively I knew I was 'way out on a limb'. My ascent had taken me eight hours, it was 16.30pm and I was alone on top of the Eiger with a possible storm coming in. I was not sure of the way down and my clothing would be suspect in bad weather. I had no torch, the only food I had was the half eaten bag of wine gums and the only people who knew where I was, were themselves many hours from getting down.

Sheer determination had got me to the summit but I knew my greatest challenge still lay ahead and that most climbing accidents happen on the way down. And that none of this would mean anything unless I got back safely. On finishing the photos I put the camera away, picked up my rucksack and started to descend. After all the months of planning and dreaming, all the effort and time involved, I had spent less than five minutes on the summit, and had not even sat down.

The way down suddenly looked unfamiliar and almost immediately I started to veer off route. I soon realized I was being forced down towards the right hand side of the face, the very area the Swiss shop manager had told me to avoid. Shortly afterward I knew I was committed to its descent, as re-climbing to look for my ascent route would take too long. I kept to the side of the snow slopes and initially things were reasonably straightforward. However, I was forced more and more onto rock buttresses, which took time and care to descend.

My ice axe, a bright orange long walking axe that I had borrowed from Rob, was becoming extremely useful for lowering myself down the rock faces. I would lean forward, jam the axe into a ledge and lower my weight onto it. The descent went on and on. After about two hours the rocks began to steepen. I began to take more chances, jumping down up to ten feet at a time onto snow or scree, all the time aware of the need to keep going. Throughout this time I was enveloped by thick cloud, unable to see more than 20 yards.

It was almost impossible to do any route finding, nor could I tell how far I had come. Enveloped in my own white world, my thought came in short bursts. I began to realise that I was totally lost and no longer in control of events. I was well off the standard route and nowhere near anything described in the guidebook. This realization, suddenly led to a feeling I had never experienced before. It involved a total hardening of my senses and a complete determination to continue, whatever the cost, and for as long as necessary. I suddenly felt a surge of energy, probably adrenaline, which made me feel physically much stronger. I knew that I could and would keep at this all night if I had too. Failure simply was not an option, not only because of what it would mean but because I had mentally said 'no' to it. It was as if I had pitched my own will against fate.

About this time I also experienced a surreal interlude. 'The White Spider' tells the story of two German climbers, Franz Mayer and Gunther Nothdurft who had disappeared after climbing the Eigerwand. For years it had been assumed they had fallen down the North or South Faces, but then their bodies had been found some years later at the edge of a gully overlooking 'little frequented snow slopes' of the West Face near where I now found myself. Suddenly I was looking at a gully, which seemed to match Harrer's description. It involved a bit of scrambling, but I felt compelled to take a look and noted clear signs of, a not too recent, human presence. There were rusty old tins lying around – but nothing that could be directly linked to Mayer and Nothdurft. Then with my curiosity satisfied I returned to my immediate reality.

After a full four hours of descent I realized that climbing down the rocky crags was simply too slow. It was now 8.30pm and although it was still light I could feel the darkness approaching fast. By this stage the visibility had improved a bit, enough to see maybe a few hundred yards at a time, and it was apparent that I was descending parallel to a steep snow slope. If I could get onto the slope and glissade down using my axe as a brake I could lose hundreds of feet a minute. The downside was of course the risk of losing control, going over an edge or ending up on a glacier in a crevasse or bergshrund, which I couldn't see. I decided to take the risk.

To get to the snow slope I had to descend a very steep cliff. Half way down it became almost vertical. So I jumped the final 15ft or so onto soft snow and rolled to a halt. Thus committed, I moved out into the middle and after sitting on the snow with my axe as a break I gently pushed off. My descent was startlingly fast and sudden. Gravity worked immediately and I slid down at an ever-increasing rate. Almost immediately I started to dig my axe in and found it took a huge effort to slow down.

My supposition had been right. I was losing height quickly, but not knowing what lay ahead meant I could not relax for a moment. It was now that my decision had its consequences. As I slid down, the snow was initially fairly smooth and soft. Suddenly, however a bare patch of rock appeared. My momentum took me right over it and I could feel the damage to my bottom. In fact the seat of my trousers had disintegrated and the top layers of skin of a large part of my buttocks had been removed though at the time I felt little pain. By leaning backwards I had fortunately avoided more significant injury.

Although this incident ended my glissading I had descended far enough to know that the way down lay below some last major cliffs. I tackled these in the same mechanical way that I had all the others and soon found myself on the lower snow slopes. The time was now close to 10.00pm and it was almost dark. Because of this I could still not precisely orientate myself in relation to the Eiger Glacier station. I knew I was down the main part of the face but worried about missing the station in the dark and ending up far below into the valley.

It took another 30 minutes to discover the answer. Just as it became completely dark I recognised the path I had started up some 15 hours earlier and, rounding a corner, I saw the lights of the Eiger Glacier station. Despite my fatigue I remembered my manners and stopped at the tent of the English lads.

'Congratulations, and just to let you know I'm back too,' I managed.

They looked exhausted and one was bandaging a badly cut hand by torchlight.

'Yeah we saw you coming down those slopes,' he said. 'I cut my hand abseiling, got caught by a rock.'

We didn't talk for long and I was soon back in the toilets at the Eiger Glacier station. On reaching my chosen place of rest I realised for almost the first time that day that I was very thirsty. In fact, my water bottle was still almost full from when I had filled it that morning. I drunk its contents and felt better. Then after lying down for a few minutes the Swiss station manager came in and beckoned me into an adjacent office room. I wasn't sure what to expect but he let me know I could sleep in here for the night and within minutes, I was unconscious.

Sometime in the middle of the night, I awoke with a start. I felt a burning thirst, as never before. Automatically I emptied a litre of water down my throat, then another and another. I had never drunk so much water so quickly. Then almost as quickly I went back to sleep. In the morning I awoke to sunshine and the dim realisation that there were several station workers stepping over me in the office. They didn't seem to mind too much but I was spurred into action by embarrassment.

The day felt good, excellent in fact. I packed my things and said goodbye to the English lads. Back down in Wengen the sun was still shining and the grass was green. I returned my crampons and smiled inwardly at the thought I had done the one thing the old man had warned me not to do. Back outside I suddenly felt hungry. I had forgotten to eat the day before and now finished my last tin of ravioli. As I ate I realised my fingers were both cut and bleeding.

I made a decision to buy some plasters at a nearby chemist and sat on a wall and clumsily attempting to patch up my knuckles and fingers. As I was doing this I became aware of an elderly Swiss lady watching me intently. She offered to help and placed the rest of the plasters around my hands and fingers. It was a kind and generous gesture. I smiled at her and said

'The Eiger.'

She replied gently in English.

'You're lucky that's all the Eiger did to you.'

She was right. The day before had been a lot harder than I had expected. My inexperience had led me to make many errors and I had been lucky. I had been into a strange, exciting new world, a world of fascinating emotions, sights, sounds and challenges and had survived to climb another day.

I knew I would be back. I had photographed the Mönch and the Jungfrau rising even higher than the Eiger (13,026 ft). Although I spent many years in Dutch schools it would be many years before I would think of heights in metric terms. But seeing these other giants I vowed to myself, that one day I would return and climb them.

Down in Interlaken I had a few hours to kill before my train left late afternoon. The crampon hire had proved more expensive than I had expected, and I now only had enough money to buy a bag of peanuts. It would be my last food until I got back to Lancaster. I was also feeling the pain of my lacerated bottom. This was now suppurating badly and I was unable to sit down. On the train this became a real problem. I was forced to either stand or kneel down in front of my seat with my head on the seat. I could see people looking at me with interest, no doubt smiling at my odd behaviour. The discomfort of this overnight-journey is now one of my lasting memories.

Back in London I decided to cash a cheque and take the train back to Lancaster rather than hitchhike. As a consequence I arrived back later that evening, having been away for just over a week. Had my 'signing on' been weekly not fortnightly I would have just missed it.

Everyone in the house was smiling. This was a world before mobile phones, where long distance communication was not easy and nobody had heard from me for a week. But now fate had one more humiliation in store for me. The suppuration from my bottom had soaked right through my pants and jeans and the three had fused. I realised I could not take them off. Fortunately Sharon came up with the answer.

'For Christ's sake have a bath Nick.'

I did but it took more than 20 painful minutes soaking in hot water, jeans still on, before I could finally get them off my bottom. Sometime later I staggered down to the lounge.

'How about the pub youth?' said Rob.

In the weeks that followed I recovered as I lay on my stomach watching the Los Angeles Olympics. This was ideal therapy and gave me time to think about what had happened. Alpine climbing seemed an amazing activity, taking place, in a magical world of snow, rock and ice. The valleys, the grassy meadows, and the people had burned themselves into my mind. I recognized the dangers but, in a way, this was all part of the attraction.

I knew I needed to find some friends willing to play this exciting new 'game' with me.

'In which the author headed for a nasty shock.'

'And had a long journey back to Lancaster.'

2. Learning the hard way

London was bathed in sunlight as we sat out on a pub terrace overlooking the Thames. Opposite me, downing his third pint was my old skydiving mate Tony O'Flaherty, at whose parents' house I had stayed on my way to the Eiger. It was May 1987, towards the end of Margaret Thatcher's second term and the capital was buzzing with energy and yuppies. We had met up to discuss the details for another Alpine climbing trip.

'I'm up for it but what about these fixed ropes,' said Tony.

"No wucking furries." I replied. 'It's plastered with them. Besides the guide book says it's only PD and is suitable for first ascentionists.'

'So how do we get there?'

'By train, it's near this place called Zermatt.'

The mountain we were talking about was the Matterhorn, the famous first ascent of which I had known of since childhood. Tony had not needed much persuading and I knew from the start that I was pushing at an open door. We had first met in 1982 whilst we were learning to parachute at Cockerham near Lancaster. He had graduated in History a year before me, and had spent a year training to be a hotel manager in Leeds before returning to London, where he was now selling fax machines in the West End.

Tony was great fun to be with, an extroverted, gregarious character with immense charm. He was a natural-born salesman, with a keen eye for women, but he was above all a man of action for whom doing was more important than reading. Extremely strong, he ran marathons and worked out in the gym regularly, but this good work was undermined by a lifestyle, which involved burning the candle at both ends. His partying, heavy drinking and general love of life were legendary. I knew that his motivation to climb the Matterhorn stemmed partly from a desire to 'tell a good wine bar story', but also partly because of the sheer challenge of conquering one of the world's most famous mountains. We had spent years working our way through the ten skydiving categories together. During this time Tony had several 'close shaves' and I began to describe him as a cat with nine lives. We had latterly done some rock climbing in Lancaster and I knew he would be a good bloke to have along. If nothing else, we would have a lot of laughs.

Since my return from the Eiger two and half years before, a good deal had happened. Initially I had stayed on in Lancaster even after most of my friends ended up taking the dreaded plunge by coming south to look for work in London - which they all found quickly. I had decided to try and make a living by writing and stayed on in Lancaster to work on my first project. This was the story of Britain's Special Operations Executive (SOE) in the Netherlands during the Second World War.

The story of the so called 'Englandspiel' where the Germans had used captured agents to mislead SOE into thinking they were building up an extensive network in the Netherlands had never been told in English before. I had two trump cards. I spoke fluent Dutch, having spent a large part of my childhood living there, and secondly my mother had managed to acquire a set of thick volumes of the official Dutch parliamentary enquiry conducted between 1947 and 1950 into intelligence activities in the Netherlands during the war. Quite remarkably, this enquiry had not only interviewed in depth all the surviving participants, including the Dutch agents who had been dropped by SOE, but also the senior German Abwehr and SD officers involved. A few British intelligence officers had also appeared to say 'good morning' and quote the Official Secrets Act.

Then, even more remarkably, the Dutch government had published the whole enquiry including interviews verbatim. Although it was mostly in Dutch and German I could imagine the extreme discomfort of the British government at the time.

With this treasure trove of information I had the basis of a good book. Starting work in the autumn of 1984 I had the first draft ready by spring 1985, all done on a typewriter. Soon I realised I could do better by acquiring a new Amstrad computer, and persuaded my sister Annetta to lend me the money for it – to be repaid out of royalties on publication.

Whilst not working I continued to rock climb. That spring I did some of my best rock climbing, leading 'Jean Jeanie' 4c and 'Coral Sea' 5a at Trowbarrow quarry. I continued to solo a good deal too and occasionally managed to save up a few pounds for the odd parachute jump. One of the people I met around this time was a laid back bloke called Terrence Truscott, who took a room in my student house. He was a postgraduate just finishing his dissertation and we got on well.

All thoughts of the Alps that summer, though, came to nothing, after I broke my ankle rock climbing. It happened on a crag in Yorkshire where I was soloing a route called 'Choss.' About 25ft up both handholds came away in my hands and I found myself in freefall. I'm still sure I would have landed OK after my parachuting experiences but the ground was at an angle and I had 'gone through' my ankle. Then on rolling over I had also hit my head on a rock. This wound was superficial, requiring only half a dozen stitches but at the time it made things look worse than they were.

Despite the accident, I remember laughing at what seemed at the time, an amusing incident. As I fell I could see a man walking his dog along the path just in front of where I was. After landing and rolling over, I saw him running away as fast as he could. His dog, evidently more interested in what had happened to me, needed to be pulled along behind him.

My friends, who had been climbing nearby, had carried me to Bradford Infirmary where the NHS had worked its magic, but I was to spend the next five weeks in plaster. Fortunately at the time, David Gower's England, were busy winning the Ashes, and the time passed pleasantly enough. After plaster came physio, and by then the summer was as good as over. This was also the time of Live Aid, which we all watched and donated to, and Fife Aid in Scotland, which I attended.

By the autumn of 1985 rumours and stories reached the climbing grapevine of an amazing epic in South America. Some bloke called Joe Simpson had broken his leg and spent days crawling down a glacier before being saved by his mates.

I also remember a lecture at Lancaster University given by

Sir Chris Bonnington, about his recent ascent of Everest when he was very briefly the oldest person to have climbed the mountain. In those days an Everest ascent was still special and a huge audience listened attentively. We had seen Bonnington climbing in the Lakes quite often, and admired him for his ability to earn a living from climbing. He was also an excellent speaker.

One of my recurrent memories of those days is the incessant discussion we used to have on almost every subject under the sun. I remember talking about my Eiger ascent with one of the younger women students. She was sure of the immorality of what I had done. We sparred to and fro in a discussion typical of those years.

'But what about the people whose lives you put at risk.'

'Which people?'

'The mountain rescue services.'

'Well it's their job of course. They are volunteers and they're both equipped and trained for it. If nobody ever went into the mountains they would be out of a job.'

'But what if they had to rescue you from a dangerous position or go out in a storm.'

'I admit you could think of some situations where it might be risky for them, but I didn't get into those.'

'But you might have.'

'I might get myself into dangerous positions doing a lot of things in life, including driving which has a very high death rate. Am I immoral for wanting to drive?'

'And what about your family? What about them if you had died?'

'They would no doubt be very upset but I could die doing a whole load of things in life including trying to avoid all risks. The point is I am not trying to die, or get stuck in need of rescue. Intent matters here if we are talking of morality.'

'You may not intend it, but you are still risking other lives.'

'There are many more activities in life which have far more impact on others, enjoying the mountains with a rucksack on your back is hardly one of the top thousand.'

'I don't agree.'

It was an endless debate. Neither of us could convince the other.

During the autumn of 1985 I rewrote my book several times on my new word processor and set about finding a publisher. After a few rejections, I realised a better strategy was to find a literary agent. By 1986 I had found Andrew Lownie, an agent specialising in historical research who was willing to take the project on. Time passed slowly and my life was relaxed.

Looking back at this period now is like looking at a different era. Unemployment in the North of England was still a big issue and a large number of bright young people, who today would be gainfully employed, simply spent a few years on the dole, climbing and drifting. The system didn't ask any real questions.

After finishing 'Errors of Judgment', as I called my book, I set about new writing projects. A diary of a University student, a sort of Adrian Mole aged 19 followed, and I also researched and started a historical novel on Richard III. My thesis, incidentally, was yes he did it, for what he felt was the good reason of avoiding more civil war, but latterly he realised his actions had been wrong and had committed suicide at Bosworth.

During these years I read a number of climbing books, which also had a big impact on me. 'Savage Arena', written by Joe Tasker, and published posthumously in 1982, was one of the two best climbing books I have ever read, the second being Herman Buhl's 'Nanga Parbat Pilgrimage'.

Tasker's clearly written account of incredible endurance, self-discipline and commitment was an endless inspiration. He and his main companions Dick Renshaw and Peter Boardman successfully pushed the climbing envelope in the 1970s with ascents of the Eigerwand in winter, along with Dunagiri, Changabang and Kanchenjunga in the Himalayas. In the end however and tragically, Tasker and Boardman pushed themselves too far on the North side of Mt Everest in 1982.

Herman Buhl's 'Nanga Parbat Pilgrimage', which was reprinted in the early 1980s, was set in the bygone era of post-war austerity. Buhl demands respect for his incredible endurance and commitment. He is most famous for his superhuman solo climb of Nanga Parbat in 1953, one of the most difficult mountains in the world. But my favourite story was how, having got a weekend off from his wife, he cycled for almost 24 hours and 100 miles along Alpine passes, then soloed the North East face of the Piz Badile in less than five hours. This is one of the great North Faces of the Alps, on which the first ascent party a few years earlier had taken 34 hours. He then cycled back through the night, fell asleep, crashed into a freezing lake and had to carry his wrecked bike miles to a local inn. Sadly Buhl too was dead, having pushed himself too far in the Himalayas in 1957.

By mid 1986 I began to feel the lack of money. Living on supplementary benefit for two years had taught me how to get by without spending money but it also meant I couldn't travel much. Even my modest trip to the Eiger was beyond me now and I realised that my proposed plan to climb the Matterhorn would have to wait. This was re-emphasized when a group of friends including John, George and Alec visited the Alps and climbed the Wellenkuppe and did the Breithorn traverse. I worked in a University bar in order to continue to parachute but even now there was no real work to be found in Lancaster.

By the autumn of 1986 and despite my reservations, I began to think about going down to London to find a job. My writing seemed to offer no immediate prospect of money, even though 'Errors of Judgement' was being passed around publishers.

Occasionally I hitched down to the Capital to see friends and was always conscious that they had enough money to eat in restaurants and drink as much beer as they liked. Most of my friends had now left the university, girlfriends came and went and I started to feel like a left over from another era. I was 24 and students of eighteen or nineteen suddenly seemed very young. By Christmas 1986 I finally made my decision. My arrival date in London was set for 1st March 1987. My Godmother, Marion, who lived in Hornchurch offered to put me up for a few months whilst I found a job and sorted myself out.

Within a week of arriving in London, I was at work for BT, commuting every day and getting used to life in the capital. As my first pay cheques came in my thoughts turned to the Alps.

That summer I was determined to return to have a go at the Matterhorn (14,672ft), the tenth highest mountain in the Alps. My choice was determined simply by the fact that I had read a lot about it and it was a famous mountain. The only other Alpine peak I knew much about at the time was Mont Blanc, but somehow the Matterhorn held more appeal.

Tony and I determined to go in mid-August, which seemed natural enough, it being the UK's unofficial holiday month. The plan was to hire most of our equipment in Zermatt and we agreed to be responsible for our own tents and supplies. Initially it was just going to be the two of us, but then I mentioned the trip to my old acquaintance from student days, Terrence Truscott who was enthusiastic about the whole idea. Over a few pints I gave him 'the fixed ropes' and 'it's a piece of cake routine', and he signed up for the trip.

This was a massive leap of faith on his behalf, as he had never climbed in his life - not even a rock climb. Looking back I am surprised this fact did not worry me more, but we were young and confident. Terrence was very fit and strong, had a pragmatic character, and clearly welcomed this new challenge in his life. I had liked him from the start. He was a year younger than Tony and I and was working at the time for the civil service. His easy going generous nature and traditional values would make him an ideal companion in the Alps.

Tony also found a new recruit, in Margie, his girlfriend at the time. Together they were going to go Inter-Railing around Europe, and would fit the Matterhorn climb into the middle of their trip. Margie wasn't actually going to climb but would come to the Hornli Hut, for moral support. It was agreed that Terrence and I would travel out to Zermatt on a Thursday evening, spend a few days getting acclimatised before meeting Tony in Zermatt campsite at midday on the following Monday.

Our climb itself would be guided by another Robin Collomb guidebook, this time coloured red. Its route description of the North East Ridge of the Matterhorn, also called the Hornli

Ridge, made it seem rather easy with descriptions of ascents by children and even bears.

We also read up about Edward Whymper, the Victorian climber who had first succeeded in ascending the Matterhorn. Whymper was an odd character but we were full of respect for his achievements. He was 25 at the time of his Matterhorn ascent, the same age as we were, which I took as a good omen. The story of the first climb of the Matterhorn in 1865, and the tragedy which followed on the descent, is well known in climbing literature and needs no repeating here. But we knew every detail of it and longed to see the area where it happened.

By May I also had some good news from my literary agent. 'Errors of Judgement' has been accepted by Hale Ltd and would be published in early 1988. There was also an advance, along with an offer to write a new book and I was finally able to repay my sister for her generous and optimistic computer loan.

Things were indeed starting to look up. I got a new job at Philips and moved out of my aunt's flat to Croydon. London that summer was an exciting place to be. The general economic depression of the early 1980s had lifted and people had money and jobs. Culturally too things were buzzing. The music was good, films outstanding and there was a new wine bar culture where one could try to meet more sophisticated women. It seemed that a lot of my old Lancaster friends were in the capital and we met up every week. I even started to get used to the London beer. The days of living on three pounds a day started to seem very far off.

Terrence and I travelled to Zermatt by train. In those days it was our only real option as neither of us had a car and flying was expensive. Terrence amused me by quoting from his 1890 Whymper guidebook to Zermatt, and by stoically maintaining that some of it might still be relevant.

We arrived in Zermatt to clear blue skies, beautiful mountain scenery and a shock.

'Bloody Hell. Are you sure we can climb that?'

We both stood transfixed by our first view of the Matterhorn, rearing up seemingly vertically in front of us - not a

Swiss chocolate box picture, but the real thing in all its glory. I tried to sound positive.

'Hmmm don't worry its got fixed ropes all the way.'

But no amount of staring, and I tried very hard, could make the Mountain look any easier or less steep.

In fact we were experiencing what the early pioneering climbers of the mid-19th Century, including Whymper had also felt. The foreshortening effect from Zermatt makes the Swiss side of the mountain look extremely steep and utterly inaccessible. This is why the first serious attempt to climb the Matterhorn in 1857, and all of Whymper's early attempts on the mountain, had been from the Italian side.

We did the only thing we could, and pretended the mountain wasn't there and a few minutes later experienced Zermatt's odd little campsite for the first time, tucked away at the bottom of the town against the railway line. Our tent was the £20 summer-only variety again and we soon settled in after which a visit to the local supermarket for provisions revealed more concerns.

'God, this must be the most expensive place in the whole of Europe.'

A foray into the streets of Zermatt also quickly confirmed, to Terence's disappointment, that his Whymper guidebook bore almost no relationship to anything in modern day Zermatt.

We had very little actual climbing gear. Both of us had a pair of boots and a helmet, but our clothing was makeshift, low budget, and did not include anything approaching what the climbers of the day were wearing.

Then that first night a strong gust of wind hit our tent, buckling the main pole. Terrence spent four hours hanging on to it to prevent the tent from collapsing whilst I slept through it all. By morning he had affected repairs but despite this our abode resembled a ruffled groundsheet.

We knew the importance of acclimatisation to higher altitude, but neither of us really understood what this meant. For several hot days we walked around the lower parts of the valleys up to 2500m, drinking from the many streams and allowing ourselves the odd beer at the many mountain restaurants. The scenery was stunning and I think my subsequent love for this area stemmed from these few days. Even today when most of my friends are at best ambivalent about Zermatt, it remains my favourite place in the Alps. However, as far as acclimatisation was concerned, we might as well have stayed in the campsite.

And all the time, there was that mountain, towering above us. We didn't talk about it, but we both knew it was dominating our thoughts. It needed a major leap of faith to link the evidence of our own eyes with the description in the Collomb guidebook. Another unsettling thing was that anyone heading up towards the Matterhorn had to walk past the cemetery in the centre of the town, which contained many graves of those who had died on the mountain, including several from Whymper's party of 1865.

Monday morning, the day of Tony and Margie's arrival came and went and by 2pm there was still no sign of them. An hour later we made a decision.

'Sod it, let's go for it, mate.'

So we trudged up to the Hornli Hut. At the hut the guardian couldn't believe, or didn't want to believe, that we were there to climb the mountain, and sent us to the walker's side of the hut. Not realising we started to heat up some Ravioli.

We were about to learn another basic lesson about climbing in the Alps. As we had not seen a cloud in the sky since we had arrived, neither of us had even thought of checking the weather forecast. Good weather was clearly the norm for these parts in August. But the hut was quite empty and the reason soon became clear. That night a major storm hit the mountain and neither of us got a wink of sleep. By early morning some minor self-preservation instinct was making itself felt.

'It all looks a bit wet. Maybe we should go down and see if Tony is there.'

'Yeah, come up again tonight and have a go tomorrow.'

So after breakfast we descended to Zermatt to find Tony and Margie examining our tent.

'Hmmnn, thought it might be yours Kelso, very you,' said Tony brightly.

Following introductions - this being the first time Tony, Terence and Margie had actually met - a new plan was agreed. Tony was clearly desperate to get to grips with the mountain.

'What about acclimatisation mate?'

'Bollocks to that, I'm fit enough.'

That afternoon, having checked that there would be a good weather forecast, all four of us walked back up to the Hornli Hut. On the way up Tony took time to chat to a guide who was descending to ask him whether he thought that we could climb the Matterhorn. The guide looked taken aback but asked Tony how fit he felt.

'Oh very.' replied Tony.

A gesture followed which we interpreted as 'Then go for it,' and everyone laughed.

This time we managed to secure bunks in the climber's quarters. After another lukewarm meal of Ravioli, we had a drink in the hut. There was an air of menace inside. Our nervousness was not helped by a message on the notice board to the effect that two English climbers had recently gone missing, and could we keep an eye out for their bodies during our climb.

I was also confused by the guidebook's description of the early part of the route. In the space of four sentences were the following lines describing the early part of the climb,

'In good conditions the route is easy to follow from the trail of scratches, but there are several false trails. In spite of this the correct route where the rock is sound, is not at all evident.'

As I tried to get my head around this (was the route hard or easy to find?), I comforted myself with the thought that by discreetly following guided parties it wouldn't matter too much. As always in a hut before a climb, we settled in for the short night, trying not to think about the photographs we had seen on the hut wall.

Next morning was eventful. We were up at 3.30am, after a sleepless night, along with about fifty other climbers and their guides. Suddenly Tony announced that it was still dark outside. He sounded surprised.

'I'm not climbing in the dark.'

I was stunned.

'But we've got to follow the guides. It's called an Alpine start and the route finding's supposed to be very tricky for the first part.'

But there was no shifting Tony

'I'm not climbing in the dark and that's it.'

And Terrence, who had never climbed in daytime or at night, seemed to think Tony had a good point.

I had not taken this possibility into account, and had clearly failed to communicate the urgency of an early start. Neither of them had ever climbed in the Alps before and although Tony had some rock climbing experience, he had no understanding of the reasons for the famous Alpine start. I would either have to go solo or wait. So we waited around, frustratingly from my point of view until first light at around 5.30am by which time everyone else was long gone.

An inventory of what we were wearing and carrying provides an insight into our inexperience and state of mind. Tony had packed a full stove with fuel, food and a water bottle,

'In case we want to stop for a brew mate.'

He looked like a contractor on a lunch break with his blue overalls and bright red helmet.

Terrence was carrying an even smaller water bottle, and unknown to him, a somewhat larger bottle of mouthwash, which had been left in his sack. He was wearing a blue helmet and was almost 'smart-casual' for the occasion. He also carried 150ft of worn, 11mm non-waterproof rope.

I was carrying the Collomb guidebook and a small water bottle. I had on my white helmet whilst my clothing was the same unfashionable collection I had been walking around London in the previous week. We all had on full body harnesses, which we had rented along with our crampons.

Within a few minutes we came to the first tricky climb up a crack and around a corner and so within minutes we were off route and lost. We spent a long time trying to make sense of our guidebook, looking for Collomb's *'Third couloir further left.'* After an hour we stopped looking and decided to find our own way up. We crawled along dangerous ledges, up gullies with loose rock and generally toured those parts of the Lower East Face other climbers never reach. We discovered the truth of the guidebook's warning *'Accidental variations are loose, steep and always unpleasant'.* Then to our dismay after four hours of climbing we could still see Margie sitting outside the Hornli Hut.

Tempers frayed then snapped. The day was burningly hot and our water supply soon ran out. Huge boulders regularly hurtled down the East Face just a few dozen yards away from us and then, just as we were really getting fed up, we spotted a couple of German climbers up on the ridge. Thus encouraged we climbed up and suddenly found ourselves back on the main route.

With this our enthusiasm slowly returned and we started to make good progress. The middle section of the Hornli Ridge is by far the easiest part of the route and involves scrambling up reasonably easy rock. However, a few hours later, the route steepened. We were just about to start the lower Moseley Slabs and could see the Solvay hut just above. The Moseley Slabs had been named after Dr William Moseley, a 26 year old American who, ignoring his guide's advice had un-roped and fallen to his death from this point in 1879. Surprisingly, this had been the first death on the mountain since its first ascent in 1865.

The Matterhorn had witnessed many deaths since then. By the late 1980s it was estimated that more than 500 people had died trying to climb its slopes. Looking at the steep groove above, it was not hard to imagine what had happened to Moseley, and as the rock climbing ahead was about grade III we stopped to collect our thoughts. None of us had roped up during the climb, and this seemed like a good opportunity to do so. Just above we could see the Solvay Hut, which is a small wooden emergency cabin, no bigger than a garden shed and only intended for use during emergencies.

At this moment Terence suddenly announced,

'I'm going to go down whilst I still feel in control.'

I half-heartedly tried to encourage him on but he remained firm.

'No, I've had enough. Go on if you want.'

Looking back, Terrence's performance had been remarkable for someone who had never rock climbed before in his life. Tony and I briefly conferred. We were already dehydrated and it was after one pm. We had climbed about two thirds of the

Matterhorn. The hardest part was still to come. Going on would mean, at best, a night out on the mountain without water.

We made the best decision we had all day, and decided to go down with Terrence, who was already rearranging things in his rucksack. Suddenly he tensed and straitened up holding something in his hand.

'Bloody Hell, Kelso. What's this?'

I knew instantly it was a bottle of mouthwash, my mouthwash, and I tried a nonchalant reply,

'Well you never know who you might meet up here.' But there was still a hint of real annoyance in Terrence's voice. The matter rested there for the moment. We were clinging, still un-roped, to a steep rock face some 1200ft below the summit of the Matterhorn, where any slip or fall would have been fatal. It was not a place for an argument.

Our decent was painfully slow as we kept losing the route, before spotting a guided group and following them down. We had been aware of guided parties around us all day, but we now witnessed an older guide berating his client for not being able to go at the required pace. An exchange of views then ensued in which the client calmly asked the guide to stop insulting him. We experienced this apparent contempt by older guides for their clients several more times that day.

At the base of the climb there was a plaque to a young American, who had fallen to his death. This had been set up by his family and it urged those who wanted to climb here to make sure they were experienced and well equipped. I had not seen it in the morning, and now could only agree with the sentiments.

By 4.30pm we were back at the Hornli Hut where Margie was waiting. Wasting no time, we raced down to the Schwarzee, missed the last cable car, and ended up having to descend on foot all the way down the valley to Zermatt and our tent. To make things more challenging, some of the obvious paths down had been closed off and we were soon off route again, crossing fields, woods and rivers, before finally reaching the campsite in the dark at about 11.00pm. Terrence and I hadn't had any real sleep for three days and dived straight for our sleeping bags. Tony and Margie amazingly still had energy to burn, and headed off to sample Zermatt's nightlife.

The next day in the campsite we lay on the grass in the sun and analysed our failure to reach the summit. Personal differences from the day before had been forgotten and we all recognised the things that had gone wrong. We had set off too late, and we were too slow – although this was not a fitness issue. We had not known the way, nor had we really understood how to use the rope whilst on the move. We had not worked well as a team but rather as three individuals, and we had not shown the mountain nearly enough respect.

The Collomb guidebook came in for a good deal of caustic comment.

'That bastard Collomb with his third couloir on the left,' summed it up, but although the guide had certainly understated the level and difficulty of the climbing, it was a solid piece of work and not the cause of our failure.

It was Terrence who put his finger on the real problem.

'Look, its obvious guys,' he said.

'We need to learn how to climb properly. We need to do some courses, get the right gear and practise things together as a team. We were crap yesterday and lucky.'

'We've got to be able to move fast over tricky terrain.'

'Right, let's learn then.'

Margie said we were all mad, but obviously some flame had been kindled, for she would later go on to become a mountain leader herself.

There was a plus side, too. We had survived, learnt many lessons, and our enthusiasm was undiminished. We had also shown we were capable of climbing, by effectively soloing the route to just below the Solvay hut, and I now look back at this trip as a major turning point in the way we approached the Alps. The saying, 'what doesn't kill you makes you stronger,' was certainly apt.

The weather remained perfect for the next day but we did no more climbing. That last evening we all had a meal in 'Whymper's Pad' as we called it, the hotel from which Whymper and his companions had set out on their fateful climb.

'Look, we shouldn't worry about it,' someone said. 'After all, it took Whymper twelve goes and five years to climb it.'

'*And* he didn't have to cope with Collomb's instructions.'

'Yeah and what about those fixed ropes? What was all that about?'

"Aaah, shut up. We didn't need them anyway."

The beer and banter flowed. Then Terrence suddenly leaned forward.

'Now about that bloody mouthwash Kelso?'

I look back now on this period through rose-tinted spectacles. It seems a completely different era, when the natural optimism of youth still made anything seem possible. We didn't yet know what fate had in store for us, but the Alps seemed a wonderfully exciting place. 'The game' would go on.

'Lesson twenty three - finding a bottle of someone else's mouthwash in your rucksack when you are thirsty, is not conducive to good team morale.'

3. Blisters and glory

So we went back to basics and learnt how to climb. Terrence and Tony went on a weekend's rock climbing course and from the spring of 1988, we started to visit Wintour's Leap near Chepstow at weekends, a few hours drive down the M4. We practised leading and seconding, placing gear, moving together, good rope work and how to tie different types of knots. We learned to interpret guidebooks, which typically devoted three lines to a route of over 200ft, and we also learned how to read weather forecasts and maps.

Together we accumulated more and more climbing experience, learning about each other's odd habits and abilities. We were all climbing at roughly the same level, which was leading HS/VS (4b, 4c) and seconding HVS (5a). Terrence in particular threw himself into the theory behind the practice and soon became known as the 'Quartermaster' because of his growing collection of climbing gear.

As we earned more money we acquired what could be described as proper climbing gear. There would be no more climbing in ad hoc coats and trousers. Gore-tex jackets were in, as was thermal underwear. Our new gear was thoroughly tested during long wet weekends in Derbyshire and the Lake District.

It was self-evident that we would go back to the Alps that summer and we chose as our target the Gouter route on Mont Blanc (15,572ft). This appealed as it was the highest mountain in the Alps and seemed less difficult than the Matterhorn. There were two tricky areas we knew, one the 'Grand Couloir', a gully with major stone fall problem, which you had to cross, and the second was the Bosses Ridge near the summit which was an exposed snow ridge. Apart from this, the weather too could be a killer. Getting caught in a storm near the summit meant you would be in serious trouble.

The climb would also mean a visit to the famous Chamonix, with its reputation for dodgy campsites and equally squalid groups of hard climbers. We had heard a lot and were intrigued, but I was also conscious that most of the tales I had heard dated from the 1960s. What was the capital of the Alpine world like in 1988? We were determined to find out and had no qualms about combining Alpinism with hard drinking in the bars, cafes and nightclubs.

Around this time Tony met a great girl called Jane. She was just what he needed, and she wisely gave Tony the room to pursue his hobbies. At that stage we didn't take too much notice, but Jane would become a long-term part of Tony's life. Her good sense of humour would be fully tested in the forthcoming years.

Tony and I were still skydiving and that spring I had completed my two-hundredth jump at Cockerham. Tony, who was not far behind in numbers of jumps, then decided to take his parachute with him to the Alps. 'Just in case we get an opportunity' which in Tony code meant 'I'm going to go parachuting in France during my holiday.'

That spring, 'Errors of Judgement' was published and appeared in my local Dillons. It was a proud moment and motivated me to present via my agent a detailed proposal for a book on MI6's activities in the Netherlands during the war. I had plenty of material on this too from my Dutch Parliamentary enquiry and had an interesting story to tell. It seemed to me that 40-odd years after the events, this was a story that could now be told. I should have known better though; for at the time, the Spy catcher trial of Peter Wright in Australia was making headlines and the British Government had made its commitment to the Official Secrets Act clear.

The proposal was turned down by my publisher and shortly afterwards I was invited to a literary get together in Central London. As I stood drinking, making conversation with some of the other authors, I was approached by an older man who started questioning me about my sources for a book on the intelligence services. I recognised immediately what was happening and, not wishing to be 'economical with the truth', told him about the published sources in the Netherlands. There was no follow up to this incident but neither would there be a book. It was the end of my attempt to make a living out of writing.

We decided to drive to the Alps in Terrence's newly acquired VW Golf for a two-week trip. This meant that we could take more gear and allow ourselves a few luxuries, such as more underwear, some smart evening clothes and, of course, Tony's parachute.

As always before an Alpine holiday I found the final weeks beforehand particularly trying, and I spent my working days 'going through the motions' as my mind was dominated by thoughts of that white, magical landscape which awaited us.

Finally, the Saturday of our departure came and Terrence and I went to pick Tony up. We found him fast asleep and hung over from some major works bash. He hadn't even packed yet.

'Yeah, sorry guys, it won't take me five minutes.'

An hour later we set off and had to push some speed limits to catch our ferry.

Chamonix and Mont Blanc were both gleaming in sunshine when we arrived. We had thought more carefully about our acclimatisation plan this time and had come up with a solution, which combined both our interest in mountains and our interest in beer. This involved taking the Aiguille du Midi cable car and spending a pleasant day drinking at the top of the Aiguille du Midi, a shade under 13.000ft above sea level.

On the second day we took the cable car and train to Nid d'Aigle and climbed up the lower part of the Mont Blanc Gouter route to the infamous Grand Couloir. We were all keen to see this key obstacle. It did not disappoint, being about 50 yards wide and, as we watched, a significant amount of stone-fall tumbled down from hundreds of feet above. Across the Grand Couloir was a thick steel wire, as thick as one of those large mooring ropes that secure large ships in harbour. The gully itself was set at an angle of about 40 degrees. The key was to choose your moment, and then follow the steel wire across during a lull in the bombardment.

Although there was no need to cross, as we were going to descend back to Chamonix we could not resist the entirely pointless challenge. I set off, looking up and managed to get most of the way across before I saw the first rocks coming down. They missed me comfortably and I arrived at the other side safely. The others followed shortly and we laughed at our stupidity. Our return was made five minutes later without incident but looking back I saw a boulder - the size of a small TV set miss someone's head by inches. It was shocking to see the speed at which this rock hurtled past.

After our minor game of Russian roulette we descended back to Chamonix, happy to have acclimatised for another day and upon receiving a positive weather forecast, that evening, we decided to go for it.

Mont Blanc was one of the first major Alpine mountains to be climbed, back in 1786. This was partly due to its relatively easy approaches, and partly also because of a monetary award, which was offered to the first people to climb it, by a local scientist.

The first successful ascent had been made up the Boissons Glacier and although its successor route called the Grand Mullets was still an option, we opted for the objectively safer Gouter Ridge route. This become popular during the 20ᵗʰ century and was now the busiest route on the mountain.

Over the last two centuries there have been many epics on Mont Blanc and the reported annual death toll from all causes still topped a 100 a year. My main regret in doing the Gouter ridge was the fact that we would pass less history.

Mont Blanc has a rich history of eccentrics. One of the most interesting was Albert Smith, a Victorian showman and travelling performer who had dreamed, as a young man, of climbing Mont Blanc. His climb in 1851 was the largest and most extravagant ever seen up until that point and his hotel bill included ninety one bottles of wine or beer and three bottles of cognac; a man very much after my own heart. He made the summit and then a fortune from lecturing and performing to an enthusiastic public. He even launched a board game based on his journey and climb.

Our own version of 'snakes and ladders' began as we set off early in the morning, only to discover on reaching the top of the cable car, that the train was not running to Nid d'Aigle. This added an hour's ascent to our day. We retraced our footsteps up to the Grand Couloir, a not inconsiderable climb of almost 3000 ft, and crossed it again without incident, although the menace still lurked. From here moderate scrambling up a 2500ft rock rib led all the way up to the Gouter Hut. I remember feeling quite tired after arriving at the hut, where we were lucky enough to find a free table.

We had climbed almost 7000ft in six hours and it took a few drinks to recover. As time passed we noticed more and more people arriving until the hut was almost literally bursting at the seams. We had not booked the Gouter hut, as nothing in our experience until then had suggested that Alpine huts could actually overflow with climbers. However this proved to be the case that night and after dinner the floor of the hut turned into an orgy of bodies covering every inch of floor, all hoping to get some sleep. A German woman unashamedly used my buttocks as a pillow, which was not a good move on her part as my night proved to be particularly flatulent.

We dozed on and off in that 'I've got to get up and do something really tough and dangerous in the next few hours,' sort of way.

Breakfast was at 3.30am and it was mayhem. I had learned the importance of staying hydrated and now started a practice I would continue in the future: drinking more than a litre of water before starting. Even if I have to pee within five minutes I have found that by doing this I often hardly needed to touch my water bottle during a climb. My other lesson had been to travel fast and light and so in my small rucksack I carried only a camera, a spare jumper, my water bottle, some chocolates - and for some reason which afterwards I could never understand, a large tin of corned beef, which I intended to eat on the summit as breakfast.

We set off by torch light at 4.00am, roped together for the first time on an Alpine peak, and I felt a real sense of pleasure. The weather was good, we were fit and on our way to the top of Western Europe, which was to us in those Cold War days, the whole of Europe.

The snow path was well defined and the going good, so it was easy to sink into a trance. After two hours we came to a hill barring our way and I recognised the Dome du Gouter. By now it was light and we decided to go straight up and over it even though this took extra minutes.

Shortly afterwards, we caught sight of the Vallot Hut, which very much resembles a large lorry container dumped on the hillside. I knew also it had a rich history, having initially been built as an observatory in the 19th century, and that all the original wood for the building had been carried up by porters and guides, a mind-boggling effort. It was only supposed to be used as an emergency hut for bad weather, but it was obvious that this was being ignored.

Another hour took us to our final test, the Bosses Ridge. I remember it being a few feet wide with sharp drops on both sides. On the French side you could just about see where you might end up, but the Italian side simply dropped out of sight. This was emphasised by Tony's water bottle, which popped out of a side pocket and fell down the Italian side. Within seconds it was gone from view.

As the Ridge came to an end I felt a growing sense of excitement. We were actually going to make it. All those months of planning, preparation and dreaming were going to be rewarded. And even more pleasing, our ascent would be 'by the book' and not a desperate high risk solo effort.

Some 20 minutes later we stepped onto the summit of Mont Blanc, which is both long and wide and could almost accommodate a 5 a side football pitch. This was just as well as we had to share it with half the caravan of climbers that had set off from the Gouter Hut four and a half hours earlier.

The view was relatively disappointing and limited because of the lack of steep drops around the top itself. You could see mountains far away glistening in the early morning sun but things closer to home were obscured. But it didn't matter too much, and made no real difference to the way we felt. After busying ourselves with taking photographs, I sat down to eat my special breakfast. Remarkably, I managed to force down half the tin before giving up. Even more surprisingly it stayed down!

I looked at my companions and could see that they were experiencing the same emotions I now felt. It had been a good team effort and represented our first real summit together.

Technically speaking, we had already climbed the Aiguille du Gouter and the Dome du Gouter but we had not counted these.

As we sat on the summit, Terrence mentioned something about suffering from blisters. He had bought some new climbing boots for this trip and they were giving him trouble. At the time it barely registered amongst all the other impressions. I sat mesmerized by a beautiful French woman celebrating her arrival on the summit.

We stayed on the summit for about half an hour. As we left I looked down across our route and was struck by the mixture of rolling hill-shaped domes of snow and jagged rock peaks. The sun glinted off the snow and ice, imprinting the view on my mind to such an extent that even now almost a quarter of a century later I can still see it. How could I ever describe or explain this to those who thought what we were doing was insane or even immoral?

Our descent started quickly but then progressively slowed as time went by. This was mainly due to Terrence, whose blisters were turning from a nuisance to something more serious with each hour that passed. We descended the steep buttress below the Gouter Hut and crossed the gully of death for the last time, again witnessing several near misses. Some people certainly seemed to have an odd sense of timing about when to cross. To my amazement I saw that the steel cable had been sliced in half and now hung in two strands down the rock face.

Sometime later Terrence ground to a complete halt. He decided to take his boots off and continue the descent wearing his inner boots only. He was clearly in a great deal of pain and was limping badly. We lacked any real first aid equipment to help him; another lesson learnt the hard way. Fortunately, the train from Nid d'Aigle was working again and we finally reached our campsite in Chamonix by about 5.00pm.

'Christ, look at that.'

We were examining Terrence's heels. The damage was far more than just blistering. He had badly lacerated heels, with the wounds going deeper than I had ever seen before.

'It hurts like hell.' was Terrence's only comment.

How he had been able to walk at all was a mystery. After a

visit to the chemists we patched things up as best we could but Terrence could only walk in open sandals, and it was clear he would not be climbing anything for a while.

Neither were Tony and I. The next day we headed for the beaches of the Riviera where we spent most of the rest of our holiday and during this time Tony managed to use up one more of his 'lives.'

True to his word, he had brought his parachute along in the car. At our beachfront campsite he then decided to try and impress some of the local girls by taking it out and repacking it on the beach. This soon had the required effect, as a group of bikini-clad young women gathered round to watch as Tony explained how to fold the chute. There was a lot of laughter, questions and smiles, mixed with 'piss-taking' comments from my side.

Two days later, at 7000ft, he jumped from a Cessna 206 at a French parachute centre. I remember watching from the plane as his chute, the very same, failed to open properly. Fortunately his reserve parachute, which he had not repacked on the beach, did. We laughed a lot about that one afterwards.

But the main lesson of the holiday, however, was not beware of French women on the beach, but never ignore blisters and take immediate action if they occur.

During the spring of 1989 our climbing trips to Chepstow became more and more frequent. I remember we climbed 'Zelda' and 'Greta' amongst many other routes. I had just split up with my latest girl friend, and Terrence was also at that time unattached, so we had plenty of free time on our hands. Tony, as always, made his own free time.

It was also during this time I developed the most effective fitness training regime I have ever known. The house in which I was renting a room had a straight flight of stairs and my housemates tolerated my using them to train on. I would sprint up and down the stairs ten times then recover by walking up and down ten times. The first time I felt I would collapse after five repetitions but over time I could do this up to 350 times in less than 90 minutes. As a consequence by the summer of 1989 I was fitter than I had ever been in my life. I was literally doing 3000 feet of ascent and descent every training session.

We sounded each other out on our summer objectives.

'I was thinking of the Matterhorn again.'

'Me, too.'

'We'd need to do some acclimatisation climbs first though.'

We would be going back to the Alps, for two weeks this time, cramming ourselves, and our gear into Tony's Peugeot 206. I told nobody at work what I was planning because I was sure they would not understand and think me a dangerous oddball. My colleagues were good people but we lived in different worlds and I was determined to keep work and personal life separate. My housemates were vocal enough.

'You're mad, Kelso,' was their usual refrain and I was frankly tired of trying to explain what I didn't fully understand myself. It was just easier to talk about other things.

We drove through the night and from the moment I had seen the mountains of the Valais in the distance I began to feel really alive. Pink Floyd's 'Dark Side of the Moon' was playing on the tape and our banter ceased as we absorbed the moment. By late afternoon we were happily installed in our usual spot in the Zermatt campsite and ready for some cold beer.

We decided to do a training climb and spent the first day ascending the Mettlehorn, which at 11,200ft towers more than 5,000ft above Zermatt. The climb is ideal for its purpose, long and easy, with the Trift Hotel nicely placed for a beer on the way back. It took us 10 hours to get up and down and we felt stronger as a result. Our fashion sense for the occasion was typical '80s with loud colourful Bermuda shorts and bright T-shirts, and we even remembered to 'slap up' properly to avoid sunburn.

The following day we took the cable car to the Trockner Steg and then struck out across the Oberer Theodul Glacier. Our objective was to get to the Theodul Hut. This was our first experience of a glacier and we were well roped up. Along the way we caught sight of a great many worrying things, rucksacks frozen into the ice and all kinds of discarded equipment. Fear of crevasses prevented us from deviating from our route but this did not stop Tony, who was leading, from promptly falling into one. Fortunately he didn't go in deep and we were soon on our way again.

The Theodul Hut was, at the time, at the top of a rock summit, which had a steep path leading up to it. It was built at the main crossing point between Zermatt and the Italian village of Breuil, on an historic pass. The hut seemed very civilised and we ordered a full meal and breakfast. We were up early and set off for the Breithorn just after 5.00am. An hour or so later we came up level with the ski slopes that lead off from the Kleine Matterhorn. We were rather surprised to find people skiing in the summer and I remember a strong feeling that I was glad I was climbing.

The views were stunning and the climbing easy. After two and a half hours we reached the summit of the Breithorn for the first time. It was bitterly cold but the views we had more than made up for it. I really like the summit of the Breithorn. It is just right, being long and broad with enough room to sit comfortably and accommodate a number of people without stress. Although it was tempting to take the cable car down from the Kleine Matterhorn we returned back down past the Theodul Hut and the Oberer Theodul Glacier.

That afternoon we spent lazily in the sun. During the evening we stumbled upon the North Wall Bar for the first time with its cheap beer and good pizzas. Since then, I've always made a point of visiting it every time I go to Zermatt.

We now felt acclimatised and fit. Our next objective though meant leaving Zermatt. Both Tony and Terrence were keen to get to grips with the Eiger West Face.

'You managed it Kelso, so it can't be that difficult.'

'Ha ha just wait.'

So we packed up, walked down to Tasch with all our gear and drove 'round the block' to Grindelwald, normally a journey of about three to four hours which Tony's driving almost cut in half. From here we took the train direct to the Eiger Glacier station. Nothing much seemed to have changed in the five years since I had last been there. The West Face looked just as unpleasant and intimidating, whilst the glacier station toilets were almost as I had left them; that is to say spotless.

There was however one difference this time - the café bar was open and we were able to spend the evening drinking cokes and studying the guidebook, still incidentally Collomb's little blue book. I have no doubt that we would have acquitted ourselves well the next day, but that evening a major storm blew up and was still blowing by morning. We walked about looking gloomily up at the clouds which still obscured the route and reluctantly accepted the inevitable.

Somehow this setback energised us as never before. Looking back I am amazed at the burst of enthusiasm, that followed, but the fact is that twenty-four hours later we would be standing on the summit of Monte Rosa's Dufourspitze.

We descended to the car, after which Tony got us back to Tasch, if anything, even faster than he had driven the day before. On arrival back in Zermatt, we re-established ourselves in the same spot of the campsite as we had been the day before and said 'hello' to all the people we had said 'goodbye' to so recently. Whilst I cooked lunch, Tony and Terrence went to check the weather forecast, and find out what the local guides advised about the Dufourspitze, which I had suggested as our next route. They returned shortly, and to my relief, said that the advice was positive.

We packed up and set of for the Gornergrat railway. At Rotenboden station we headed off, traversing downwards towards the Gorner and Grenz Glaciers. These offered another new experience, that of being on a dry glacier. We amused ourselves on the way by jumping across the crevasses, and even bridging them for photographs.

The Monte Rosa Hut was busy but not excessively so. In those days it stood a good deal closer to the ice than now and had a nice terrace overlooking the glacier. We set off at 3.00am by head torch, following a procession of climbers, some guided, some not, but all plodding upwards at a steady rate. The Dufourspitze is the longest climb, from the hut to the summit, of any mountain in the Alps. It is also the second highest mountain in the Alps. Collomb had graded it F+ and made it sound easy and despite our reservations about his grading we felt confident.

The first part of the route is a scree slope after which you come to the glacier. Crossing onto this caused a few interesting moments as the bergshrund was both deep and wide. After that it was just hours of plodding as we steadily gained height. Tony began to slow down which was a remarkable story in itself.

At sea level Tony was the strongest person I knew. He was a good runner capable of three-hour marathon pace, which he combined with good upper body strength and a strong, very determined character. However, above 13,000ft his strength seemed to dissipate and it was mainly willpower that kept him going. This was not just a matter of acclimatisation; it seemed to be something in his 'body make up'. It was a startling realisation as I had always expected Tony to single-handedly carry Terrence or myself down, should the need arrive.

That morning though we witnessed Tony's real strength of character, as he forced himself up to the summit ridge. I myself was bursting with energy and felt capable of running up the remainder of the route. Yet at sea level I knew I would not be able to hold a candle to Tony's fitness and strength. Terrence was very similar to me. He also seemed to acclimatise well and was going strongly.

The summit ridge of the Dufourspitze reconfirmed our view that Mr Collomb's guidebook was massively understated. Suddenly things got steep, exposed and nasty. I switched my mind off as I mechanically swung out on rock faces or scrambled over boulders, all the time aware that a fall on either side of the ridge would be unpleasant and potentially lethal. I was sure there were bits of grade III. We moved together in classic style, using natural protection wherever possible - another first. Then just as the ridge began to seem impossibly long, we arrived at the summit cross.

It was bitterly, bitterly cold and quite mind numbing. We took a number of photos, shook hands, and then without further discussion set off down. We had spent more than seven hours getting to the top yet had spent only two minutes on the summit. I had spent longer on top of the Eiger.

It took another four and a half hours to get back to the hut. We even spent the final half hour in a race, each having chosen a different route down the scree fields. This was a draw as we arrived at the hut at the same time.

That evening we sat in the North Wall Bar sipping large glasses of beer and feeling wearily satisfied.

'How the hell could that be graded F plus?'

'Yeah, I wonder how many people have died as a result of that guide book.'

'What we need is a new guide book written for ordinary climbers, with practical things and not written by someone who thinks its cool to under-grade everything'

'Maybe conditions have changed since he wrote it, maybe its global warming.'

It was only Thursday evening and we had been in Switzerland for six days. We all knew what we really wanted next was a 'return match' with the Matterhorn; after a good night's sleep that is.

But although our morale was by now sky high, the barometers were falling all over the Alps. We accepted this news of bad weather with good grace and decided on a brief interlude by the sea.

We could have gone to the Italian lakes, or even Venice, but Tony remembered a childhood vision of Rimini - as the place to be on the Italian Riviera, and this became our next objective. It took all day and most of the evening to get there and we slept that night in the car after arriving too late to get into the campsite.

We spent two days on the beach, unsuccessfully admiring the local Italian women. At the end of the second day I had two unpleasant surprises. Having forgotten to put suntan cream on my feet they had become badly sun-burned. So much so, I could hardly walk. I cursed myself for putting my chances of climbing the Matterhorn in serious doubt. The second surprise was a long distance phone call to the Zermatt guides office, which ascertained that the good weather was on its way.

We had planned to stay a further day on the beach but this news shook us into action and meant my feet had no time to recover. Within half an hour we were in the car, which Tony subsequently thrashed to its limits to get us back to Tasch.

We arrived late in the afternoon and as Tony and Terrence were adamant they did not want to stay in Zermatt, we decided on the novel approach of camping in Tasch - normally little more than the car park for Zermatt. In fact, the Tasch campsite by the river is actually rather pleasant.

It is interesting to note by the way, that a dislike of new developments of Zermatt is nothing new. In 1909, R L G Irving described the same phenomena during a paper given to the Alpine Club. Even then, it was fashionable to decry the new building developments of the time. The old men of the Victorian era would no doubt have fainted at the sight of modern-day Zermatt.

The next morning we headed up the valley. Although my feet were still badly burned I found I could walk without too much pain. The weather forecast was good and we stopped in Zermatt for a final lunch in civilisation.

I looked at the passing tourists and wondered how they were going to spend the next day. One of the problems was that we knew what to expect, and whilst I pretended to be nonchalant and unconcerned, inside I felt tense and nervous. It was like the hiatus before a major exam, which you could not avoid, and on which your entire future depended.

After lunch we raced up to the Hornli Hut in an hour, and arrived just in time to witness a remarkable scene. Even though it was a Tuesday afternoon, a priest in full regalia was holding a service on the wooden veranda. None of us were particularly religious but the idea of having divine blessing for the next day was appealing. So we joined the service and listened to the priest. He spoke in German, which I could translate for the others and I remember him finishing by saying:

'*And may the strong ones look after the weak ones on the mountain tomorrow.*' I had to smile. Our reaction was, I think, indicative of our state of mind, and I now empathise with the old saying, '*There are very few atheists in the trenches.*' It was my third night in the Hornli Hut before a Matterhorn climb, and it didn't get any less tense.

This time, however, we were not going to rely on our Collomb guidebook. Our plan was to follow the guided parties at least through the first part of the route. Tony, seeking even greater insurance, struck up a conversation with a French guide. He was going to take an older Japanese bloke up the ridge the next day and had offered to take his son too. The son, who was about our age, had politely refused, as he thought a 2-1 ratio too dangerous. This surprised us all and we immediately warmed to the Frenchman and struck up a lively conversation.

We had found from experience that, as a rule, the further away from a valley or mountain region a guide came from, the more open relaxed and friendly he was likely to be. The local Zermatt guides were very protective and some of them were downright hostile. Most of these were older men and we had already noticed a clear difference between the older and younger Swiss. The latter were far friendlier, open minded and cosmopolitan.

The younger Japanese told me the story of how he and his father had almost got the top of Mont Blanc when their guide, at the time had suddenly announced he had a headache and was going to go back down; they had had no option but to follow him. They had had to repeat the whole experience a few days later. We all agreed that our new French friend would be the one to follow, at a discreet distance of course.

The following morning bore no comparison to two years before. We awoke and conspiratorially kept a close eye on our targets. We breakfasted some distance away but left at the same time and kitted up alongside them. Twenty seconds after they left the hut we followed and managed to find ourselves just behind them at the first difficult crack.

Our French guide, no doubt aware that we were shadowing him set a cracking pace. I was not surprised by this, but rather by the ability of the Japanese father, who was clearly overweight, to keep up without complaining. For two hours, mostly in the dark, we did not stop. Gully followed gully and rock step followed rock step. We were still un-roped and Tony started to drop back, but Terrence and I kept going, scared to lose contact at this crucial stage. Before long we had lost contact with Tony who followed on gamely and was swept along by the guided parties following.

After just over two hours of this we reached the Solvay Hut. It had become light by now and the day promised to be a fine one. The Solvay Hut has a narrow wooden veranda and it was here we stopped for a rest. We decided to halt and wait for Tony rather than follow the guide, a decision I am now very pleased we took. Had we continued, we could have climbed the route in just over three hours, but the price would have been team unity, and that was more important.

We waited for almost 45 minutes before Tony reached the hut, although we had been shouting encouragement to him for most of that time as we could see him climbing up.

Above the Solvay Hut the route steepened immediately with the onset of the upper Moseley Slabs and we appreciated how wise our decision had been to retreat two years earlier. The climbing became more exposed than before and we stopped to rope up and put our crampons on. At regular intervals there were metal stanchions, which we could run the rope around and which gave us some basic protection.

We now met a new problem. Because of the time we had waited, many groups had either passed us or were already on the way down.

A shout came from below. It was Tony who had suddenly started swearing as one of his crampons had broken, not the strap but the metal itself. There was nothing we could do, so Tony went in the middle of the rope and we now experienced some of the famous Hornli Ridge 'traffic jams' - climbers ascending trying to pass those descending - which slowed us up considerably. There were now so many people above that I decided to put my helmet on. Shortly after this we finally reached the fixed ropes that we had read so much about. These were huge things designed, it seemed, to tether supertankers. I quickly noticed that they were very difficult to hold; hands even without gloves tended to slip down them.

Despite their awkwardness, we still ended up using them quite often, more for the sake of speed than the difficulty of climbing. I had just pulled up onto a small ledge when I heard a scurrying above me. Instinctively I pushed my head forwards and then felt a couple of crampons land on the top of my helmet as a woman abseiled straight onto my head. Without my helmet I would probably have had 16 neat holes in my skull. The ledge barely fitted the two of us and the woman, who was American, kept apologising over and over again for what had happened. I told her it didn't matter, that I understood, held no grudges, that's what helmets were for etc, and anything else I could think of to pacify her for she was clearly very upset.

We continued climbing the steep ridge overlooking the North Face. The exposure below was quite mind numbing. It could not fail to cross my mind that it was close to here that Whymper's four companions had fallen to their deaths in 1865.

The fatal slip had come from an 18-year-old Englishman, called Douglas Hadow, with little climbing experience, and I wondered what Terrence was thinking. Outwardly he looked his usual relaxed and laid-back self, but only two years earlier he had been even less experienced than Hadow.

Finally we reached the top of the final buttress and the terrain became snowy and more easily angled. I continued to lead up the final slopes and after another fifteen minutes we could sense we were close. Then, at 9.30am, we stepped onto the summit ridge.

My emotions were complex, with elation mixed with disbelief and tension. This was the moment I had dreamed of for so long, the realisation of a dream. Yet I did not feel as I had imagined. Deep down I was pleased, very pleased but I was also very conscious of being only half way. In the back of my mind was the nagging thought that we still had to descend those cliffs. Hundreds of climbers before us who had reached this point, and had no doubt congratulated themselves, had never made it down to Zermatt to celebrate that evening.

The summit of the Matterhorn is long and thin and exposed. On the one side you have an interesting view all the way down the North Face. On the other side you sense the view all the way down the West Face. The border between Switzerland and Italy runs through the summit and in the middle of the ridge is a dip where the famous summit cross can be found. We knew that the Swiss end is slightly higher than the Italian end and this is where we stayed. For once we were in no hurry and sat down to admire the view.

It was a perfect day, with no wind and an unimpeded view across the Alps. This was no Mont Blanc summit view. You could see everything both close up and far away.

We chatted with some Italians including one very vocal lady, and although we were more British about things we felt the same inside. This international sense of companionship allowed me to relax for a few moments. With hindsight I wonder how Douglas Hadow must have felt back in 1865. With little or no climbing experience he had scaled one of the most difficult mountains in the Alps. Had he allowed himself to feel relaxed and happy during the hour he spent on top or was his mind already worrying about getting down?

Our own turn came soon enough and we braced ourselves for by far the most dangerous and difficult part of the day.

'Come on chaps, total bloody concentration.'

'Don't be so dramatic. We'll be fine.'

The first part was straightforward to the top of the cliffs. Tony went first on a tight rope because of his one crampon. We started down the cliffs, using the fixed ropes and stanchions on the way. Mostly we climbed together but occasionally we lowered each other down. The exposure seemed worse going down and we were forced to confront it constantly. Any unprotected slip here would have been fatal. The only thing to do was to keep going as safely as possible. I set myself the mental target of reaching the Solvay Hut. Once here I knew we could do the next bit. It took more than 90 minutes and at times I was stretched further than I wished.

At the hut we rested for a short while. We still needed to concentrate even though the worst part was over. Below us were the lower Moseley Slabs and we agreed to un-rope once we had passed these. I remember little of the rest of the descent even though it took another three hours.

Gradually I fell behind the others. For some reason I have never been able to descend anything quickly, whether it is an easy snow slope or the Hornli Ridge. In some ways though I preferred to do the last part alone. I was lost in my own world, trying hard not to think about having made it, but unable to entirely suppress growing feelings of elation. Finally I swung down the rope of final crack to the snow at what had been the start of the climb proper and felt the tension draining away.

Before going down to the Hornli Hut, I sat for a few moments looking back up at this magnificent mountain and felt a very deep sense of satisfaction. One day in the future, no doubt, this fantastic rock spire will collapse, as nature continues its relentless attrition, and the world will be the less for it.

'Ah, there you are Kelso. We were starting to get worried.'

I could see Tony and Terrence ensconced in the corner of the hut with big grins on their faces. They were half way through a bottle of beer each and had one waiting for me. It was good to be back safe, drinking a toast with two very good mates.

'Congratulations guys, great effort.'

'Thanks for waiting for me at the Solvay Hut. I really appreciate that.'

'No worries, I wrecked my boots coming down that last bit.'

'Who's for another beer?'

Our celebrations at the hut however were brief. Mindful of not wanting to miss the last cable car, as we had two years before, we set off down at a rate of knots. This time we made it with minutes to spare and soon found ourselves walking through Zermatt. I could hear the 'Pet Shop Boys' singing in the background about 'looks, brains and lots of money.' We were back.

Now came the tiring bit. For some reason we had no money with us and were forced to walk down to Tasch campsite, carrying all our gear. It was stiflingly hot and the road seemed to go on forever, but about two thirds of the way down I heard a car coming and automatically stuck my thumb out. The driver stopped and we all piled in gratefully.

That was the end of the climbing. We considered the Eiger again but the timings for our ferry just didn't work out. I was conscious of being on a massive natural high, which I think we all shared. This was not a fleeting feeling but would last for months and provide a continuous low-level sense of satisfaction and achievement.

We motored back across rural France taking our time and avoiding the motorways. I remember one ten-course meal, provided by an elderly French lady in a small village restaurant, as the best I have ever had. That night we discussed philosophy over some good wine, until late into the night, and then went and biviied on a grass lawn in the middle of the village. Next morning we awoke to find some dogs sniffing us whilst the locals kept a safe distance.

We had learned to climb in the Alps, to play 'the game,' and despite our inauspicious start a few years earlier, had become an effective team. We were in the prime of life, young and fit, and still without the responsibility of having a family and children. Questioning the morality of what we had done in the mountains simply didn't occur to us at the time. It wasn't an issue.

I had also achieved my dream of climbing the big three names in the Alps and was unsure what to do next. Tony and Terrence, however, still wanted to climb the Eiger and this would lead to another eventful year.

'*And then the author received an unexpected scalp massage.*'

4. Team ID is born

After our Matterhorn success I spent the autumn of 1989 on a naturally induced high, which was given a boost in November by the news of the fall of the Berlin Wall. Within an hour of the news breaking my housemates and I tried to get a flight to Berlin to join the party but we were already too late. However there was enough partying to be done in London. This was the time of the Lawson boom and money seemed to be everywhere, particularly in London.

House prices were rising at an unprecedented rate and for the first time in my adult life, real personal economic progress could be imagined. The next few years would see the world change radically. In the words of one thinker, it was 'The end of history as such' and soon, the world would no longer live with the threat of an imminent nuclear holocaust.

That autumn we visited the Mile End climbing wall for the first time. In those days it was less organised, and in many ways more fun. It gave us a place to meet up with other friends and was to become a major part of our social lives in the years to come.

We had decided on returning from the Alps that we would go on a major trip to Africa in the summer of 1990 to climb Kilimanjaro and Mt Kenya. The team for this trip grew during the year with Tony's girlfriend Jane joining us; then John and Liz decided to come too.

I had known John Carpenter and Liz Peters, as she was called then, since 1984. They had met at their university mountaineering club and their relationship had thrived over the years despite many physical separations. John had taught geography at a grammar school for a number of years but had now joined a fast track scheme at Barclays Bank. He loved the outdoors and was most at home reading a map of some soon-to-be-visited mountain range.

Liz was a good climber too with a keen eye on safety and a firm view for anyone taking unnecessary risks. Unusually amongst my friends, she has a strong religious faith and was a regular churchgoer, although we never, to my recollection ever really discussed it. She was a scientist, a crystallographer, who was, at the time, involved in research work at Birkbeck College in London. Here she knew a fellow scientist called Jerry Baum, who was also doing research. Jerry had a dry sense of humour. In his younger years he had been a champion sprinter, but now he needed to work on his fitness. He was also very enthusiastic about Kilimanjaro and became the final member of the group.

That autumn, I passed my driving test and acquired a Renault 5. After Christmas, I drove it to Fort William to meet up with John, Liz and Terrence and we walked up Ben Nevis almost getting lost at the top in the cloud. During the descent Terrence suffered a freak injury, when he managed to slip backwards and impale his arm on his ice axe. It was a nasty wound, which needed hospital attention, more amusing afterwards than at the time. Together we celebrated Hogmanay with real whisky and toasted in the 1990s.

For me the new decade started badly. My grandfather, to whom I had been very close, died on New Year's Eve. I remember the long stories he told me as a child of his working class life in Northern England during the early part of the 20th century. He had a passion for sport and would no doubt have enjoyed rock climbing had he ever had the chance. Our generations represented a major dividing line in our history and "you don't know you're born" was his favourite phrase. He loved life and I still miss him to this day. Then, on my way to his funeral in Manchester, I had a car accident when someone rammed me from behind.

After this difficult winter, we spent a good deal of time climbing at Chepstow. Both Tony and Terrence were becoming as obsessed by the Eiger as I had been five years earlier. It dominated a lot of our thinking and I was up for another go.

It was decided that, even though we were going to Africa for three weeks in July and August, there would be time for a week in the Alps in early July. Shortly before we were due to travel, I met up with Mark Phillips, an old friend from student days, with whom I had rock climbed in the quarries around Lancaster in the mid 1980s.

Mark decided to join us and put his company car at our disposal. He was a Northerner with a degree in Engineering from Cambridge, and at the time was working for a firm of consulting scientists and engineers in London. He had made a presumed first British ascent in the Altai Mountains of southern Siberia with another friend, Alec Erskine in 1988, something that gave him huge credibility in our eyes. After this he had also spent six months cycling by himself to China, right through Europe and along the Karakoram Highway. He had many stories to tell about his time on the road. I remember one being about how he had been looked after by a kindly Chinese family when 'he was rather poorly'.

We drove to Grindelwald in the first week of July. Three days before our departure I had come down with flu and, despite spending this time in bed, I was still not a well man in the back of the Sierra. Consequently, I took little pleasure from proceedings on the way but perked up a little at the sight of the Eiger again. I may not have felt great, but I was confident that after months of stair training my fitness level was high.

For the first time since my first visit to the Alps in 1984, the weather was not good on arrival. This was quite surprising, as we had blithely assumed that the usual blue skies and sunshine, which we had experienced for most of the last three trips, would still be present. We spent a day waiting in a damp campsite near Grindelwald before things started to improve, then made our way up to the Eiger glacier station. I was still not feeling fully recovered and travelled on the train with the bags whilst the others walked up to save money and have some exercise.

On arrival at the by now familiar glacier station, we discovered that the food bag had somehow been left behind in all the excitement and the cafe was not open. We shared the small amount of food we did have, about a quarter of a tin of corned beef and a few mouthfuls of mashed potatoes. It was hardly the ideal preparation the night before a major climb.

I had brought a new video camera and planned to film our

ascent. This was not one of the sleek lightweight digital things we have today but a bulky, heavy analogue number, which ran on tapes and batteries of limited life. At the time however it was high tech, and would provide me with another challenge during the climb.

Early next morning I had a sense of déjà vu as the weather looked ominous and we decided to delay our departure. By 9.00am we were still loitering around the tents and a clear decision should really have been taken to quit for the day. However at 9.15am the sun suddenly appeared and the four of us decided to set off, uncertain as to whether this was a serious attempt or just a bit of exploring around the lower slopes.

We were still using Collomb's guidebook and decided to follow the route it described rather than take the rock buttress direct, which I had done six years earlier. This meant climbing to the right, up a series of gullies and couloirs. Gradually we gained height although everything seemed far harder than I remembered. The rock itself was heavily verglassed and we needed to take care for although we were climbing together, we were not roped up at this stage.

After a few hours of this we reached the viewpoint over the North Face, about a third of the way up the route. From here things got snowier. The lads consulted me constantly.

'Is this the right way Kelso?'

'I can't remember.'

'What was it like last time then?'

'I can't remember.'

'I don't believe you ever climbed this damned mountain.'

I had not expected to remember so little of the detail, but a lot of things now seemed different.

One thing we did little of was filming. My plans, so easily thought out at home, had me using the camera every five minutes to film anything that looked the least bit interesting. In reality I lacked the energy, partly because I was still feeling the effects of my recent flu, to even open my rucksack and get the camera out.

It was further confirmation that conditions are everything in the Alps and that they could transform a mountain from an easy grade into something far harder. Had the conditions been like this in 1984 I doubt I would have made it. We roped up for various bits and continued past various tricky gullies before finally emerging onto the upper slopes, which were covered in deep snow.

By this stage I was starting to lag behind the others as we slowly fought our way up. I also noticed that the weather was turning fast with heavy clouds coming in towards us. I could see the others sitting waiting on a rock about 50 ft away and during the ten minutes it took to reach them, the cloud reached us.

We discussed the situation.

'It's getting late lads,' said Mark. I looked at my watch and was shocked; it was 3.30pm.

'How far do you think it still is?'

'It can't be too far now. It would be easier to see if this cloud wasn't moving in.'

At that moment the weather started to turn, the wind got up and it started to snow lightly.

'If we go on, we'll be biviing,' Mark commented, 'and it looks like it's turning nasty.'

This last was the key. We had no bivi gear with us, and none of us really fancied sitting out a night in a famous Eiger storm. I felt far from well and knew we would anyway have a fight to get down. Reluctantly, we decided to retreat even though we were in fact only about 150m from the summit.

The snow soon turned to hailstones and I remember watching Mark abseil down a cliff with eyes screwed tight. It was now, for some reason, that I remembered the video camera and managed to film Tony dramatically descending the same way moments later. It was indeed dramatic footage, but it was also almost the only bit I took on the whole climb.

Climbing down was harder than going up, and we had to face inwards and kick steps down many long slopes. Caution was needed and the concentrated effort required was almost as draining but, despite this, I felt we were well in control of the situation. There was none of the adrenalin-pumping desperation of my decent six years earlier. We had a rope, we were now experienced climbers and there were four of us.

After about three hours of this, during which time the weather did not let up for a moment we reached the area of the ledge where we could see the North Face. As we slowly descended a tricky bit of ground I was aware of the snow turning to ice. We were un-roped at this stage and I noticed that Tony was not wearing his crampons, which he had taken off during the descent of the snow slopes. I was just about to say something when Tony took a step on to the ice and slipped.

He started sliding, face down, quite slowly towards me. For a few moments it seemed as if the world was in slow motion. As Tony slipped past me I made a grab for his helmet and got a grip on something only to find it was his sunglasses, which suddenly ripped off from under his helmet, leaving me holding a pair of fine shades but nothing else.

We watched stunned as he continued to slide at this slow but steady pace towards the drop below. Tony had also dropped his axe so had no way to stop himself and he was now beyond our help. Had he had either crampons or an axe he would have stopped himself immediately, but now he had neither.

Someone shouted, 'STOP YOURSELF!' I watched in horror as he slid down, face inwards and spread-eagled, towards the edge of a huge cliff. Going over the edge would mean certain death, and he was now only a few feet from the edge. Then, just when all seemed lost, he managed to jam his right foot into a patch of snow, which finally stopped his slide. He was literally on the edge of the cliff and another second would have seen him go over. A few moments later his ice axe flew down the slope towards him and, unbelievably, Tony looked as if he was going to make a lunge for it.

'LEAVE IT!' shouted Mark.

The axe duly disappeared into the void, the last we ever saw of it - it must have fallen more than 500ft.

For a few seconds nobody said anything or even moved. We all felt stunned by what we had just witnessed. Then, quickly, we recovered and threw the rope down to Tony. Together we pulled him up and Terrence set about helping him to put his crampons on. Tony was clearly in mild shock as we roped up.

With crampons on, the ground was fairly straight forward,

and we made progress down and away from the danger zone. Nobody said anything and we needed to set up three more abseils, one down a waterfall, in order to get to the easy snow slopes below.

I remember looking back up the route we had descended and thinking, no way is that PD. It had been one of the hardest afternoons I had ever had and we had been extremely lucky not to lose Tony on the way down.

Then just as we had emerged onto the easier ground below, the clouds and snowstorm disappeared and the sun reappeared. It was as if the Gods had been testing us, and had now lost interest in their cat and mouse game.

We sat down and reflected on what had happened.

'My God, I thought you were a gonner there,' said Mark. 'You were bloody lucky Tony,' added Terrence.

'You'll need to get yourself another ice axe.'

'Yeah it kind of gave its life for you.'

We all laughed and slapped him on the back, but in truth things had been too close for comfort and there was a forced cheerfulness about our banter. The lesson was obvious: always wear crampons. Tony had used another of his lives and I remembered how he had climbed the Matterhorn with only one crampon the year before. Had this lead to over-confidence?

We got back to our tents just before dark and slept fitfully, being four persons in a three-man tent. Half way through the night this eased as Mark, who had a bivi bag decided to sleep outside at the Eiger glacier station.

The following day I began to realise that, despite the lack of sun for most of the previous day, my face was extremely sunburnt. This was not just a bit red but swollen, puffy and suppurating. I had never been so burnt and it recalled some of the postcards I had seen of 19th century travellers on glaciers with their faces looking like raw meat. It was another lesson almost learned; always slap on the sun block, even if the sun is not shining.

For the rest of the week the weather worsened and we headed off to Chamonix. Here we found a bar called the Jeckyl and Hyde and spent two long nights celebrating Tony's survival.

On the second night we met up with Mal Duff, who was leading a group of clients on a three week Alps trip. He was very opinionated on all aspects of the British climbing world and seemed to dislike a large number of well-known individuals. But we enjoyed his company that night. There was a karaoke machine, the first one any of us had ever seen, and everyone in the bar had a go at our bottle walking game.

There was also a bloke from the Belgium equivalent of the SAS who had a long chat to Tony, then invited him on the Belgium Cho Oyu expedition for 1992. He seemed serious and Tony was well chuffed.

At about 3.00am, Duff and his party finally left, with Mal looking far from happy. Terrence was sitting at the bar with an enigmatic smile on his face.

'You know, I think the barman has put our drinks on Mal Duff's tab,' he said finally.

'Shit shouldn't we say something, we've had loads.'

'Too late. He's already settled up and gone and anyway I've just heard what his clients were paying him for this trip,' said Tony.

We never did get a chance to make amends. Some years later we learned the sad news that Mal Duff had died leading an expedition on Everest.

Later that morning we sat at the bar with the barman, a young Swedish bloke, who was running the establishment with his girl friend. Tony was telling him the story of how he had almost fallen off the Eiger just a few days before. The barman looked serious.

'I've known many guys come in here for a drink and then I hear later they have been killed in the mountains,' he said.

'Ah, no chance. That's not going to happen to me,' said Tony confidently.

'Please be very careful. I wouldn't want you to join them. It is very easy to die climbing in these mountains.'

Tony laughed it off with his usual charm but the conversation stuck in my memory.

The next day Mark coined a new term for us as result of the Tony incident. We became Team ID, which stood somewhat melodramatically for Team 'Instant Death'. The name stuck and was adopted by all who knew us. In later years it was used to describe a large group of people, including wives, girlfriends and children.

Chamonix impressed me as being a fun place to be in bad weather. One evening we watched the England Germany World Cup semi-final in the Bar National. This was famous and rough in the '50s and '60s climbing world and was now mixed with British and German fans. But the humour was good, and things on the pitch were too tense for any trouble.

Later that month seven of us - John and Liz, Tony and Jane, Terrence, Jerry and I - flew to Nairobi. It was to prove one of the best trips I have ever been on. We climbed Kilimanjaro, 19,340ft, by the standard route and spent almost a week on Mt Kenya failing to climb Batian and having to settle for Lenana at 16,300ft. The trip was concluded with a safari and a few fine meals in Nairobi. It was during this period we learned of the Iraqi invasion of Kuwait and almost immediately we disappeared into the wilds to be out of media touch for a week, not knowing the extent of our involvement in a major war defending Saudi Arabia and whether we would return to a world without oil. My memory is of a fun trip with good friends and not a single argument during the three weeks we spent out there.

During the autumn of 1990, a new tradition started for Team ID when we participated in the Dovedale Dash in Derbyshire. This four and a half mile cross-country run, invariably in the mud, had a rich history, going back to medieval times. It also allowed us a day's rock climbing on the Saturday. At this stage, we camped in a local field without facilities and didn't mind.

We saw little of Tony during the winter of 1990/91. He had announced during the summer that he was in financial trouble after his company had gone bankrupt, owing him lots of money. He, in turn, had creditors and - by the winter of 1990 - he was keeping a low profile and living on a severely reduced budget. This state of affairs would last for more than two years.

That November also saw the fall of Margaret Thatcher. She

had been Prime Minister for all my adult life and suddenly it seemed possible that a new style of leader could, after all, run the country.

It was during the spring of 1991 that I decided to invest in a flat with my old skydiving friend Paul Taylor. Neither of us could afford our own property, and with prices rising, we didn't want to miss out on any future rises. We failed to notice, however, that the property market was about to nose dive, and within months of our purchase, we were into negative equity. Paul suffered from asthma and couldn't therefore climb in the Alps, although he would have liked to. During this period, however, he did complete the Tour de Mont Blanc and topped it all by trekking two hundred miles from Kathmandu to Everest base camp in Nepal. It was also during this period that he met Sheila who was to become his long-term partner.

Terrence and I were in-between girlfriends at this stage and we spent many weekends rock climbing on the sea cliffs at Swanage. I remember one spectacular route, which started inside a cave and traversed across the top of this cave before exiting and finishing through a borehole above.

These weekends were a relief from work where I was now the press officer for the lighting division of Philips in the UK. In January 1991 I organised a major press event in the House of Commons where we launched a new generation of energy saving light bulbs. John Wakeham agreed to attend and George Robertson, later the Minister for Defence and Secretary General for NATO, agreed to sponsor us. Being able to rock climb at weekends was good anti-stress therapy.

The First Gulf War of early 1991 dominated the news that winter. I had a direct personal interest, as a distant cousin of mine was serving in the British army at the time, and he was somewhere in the Saudi desert. In fact he would fight in the frontline during the four-day land campaign and was in an armoured vehicle only a few hundred yards from the two British vehicles, which were hit by so-called 'friendly' fire. I met him for a drink on his return and he still seemed dazed by the whole experience.

Easter 1991 saw more rock climbing in North Wales with Paul Lovatt-Smith, known by all as 'Low Fat', who had just climbed the Italian ridge on the Matterhorn. Paul had a house in Mile End just by the climbing wall, and his place would become a focal meeting point for us for some years to come.

We did some hard climbing up to HVS that weekend and I remember a visit to the café run by Eric Jones – a legendary British climber. That spring also saw the wedding of John and Liz, a grand occasion in Bedfordshire. They were a well-matched couple and had been going out for eight years by this stage, and a large number of climbing friends attended. At one point a small fire broke out in the Marquee, which actually added to the occasion.

By the summer of 1991, I was doing some of the best rock climbing of my life. I remember soloing a 70ft VS in Derbyshire with a confidence that surprises me today. Terrence and I had some serious Alpine plans for the summer, a climb of the Eiger Mittelegi ridge being one of them. Then something happened to throw all these plans out of the window.

I had met a Polish girl called Agata, and decided to spend my summer holidays with her. Terrence took the news that I would not be going to the Alps that summer well enough. It was difficult for me to tell him and I knew I was letting him down, but I also knew the Alps would still be there the next year. I often wonder what we might have achieved if we had gone that summer. We were both in peak fitness and form and the routes we were planning were a higher level than ever before.

I was, however, able to provide Terrence with some compensation. A journalist friend of mine called Marcus Gibson, was at that time working for the European newspaper. The newspaper agreed to sponsor a long weekend attempt on the Eiger for which Tony, Terrence and Marcus and a girl called Bev all signed up. Agata and I waved them off from our flat in London one Friday evening. They were back the following Monday evening to report that both Tony and Terrence had made it to the summit. It was a very fine effort in such a short time, and meant that both of them had completed the big three names. It would also prove to be Tony's last Alpine summit.

That autumn, on the 18th October 1991, Agata and I got married. She already had a five year-old son called Michael, and so I suddenly acquired a family and responsibilities overnight. As a wedding present, my parents provided us with the money to buy Paul out of his share of the flat, something that we finalised by the spring of 1992.

Our honeymoon was a weekend in Windsor as we were short of money at the time. Indeed the whole marriage cost less than £200 including registry office fees. This fitted in with my 'not being forced to follow conventions' philosophy. Agata didn't mind as, for her, it was her second marriage and in truth we couldn't have done it any other way at the time.

Agata and I spent a number of weekends going rock climbing that autumn. She had never climbed before and was suddenly seconding VS climbs. We also went walking in the Lakes and Derbyshire, and Agata was soon familiar with a number of key rock climbing areas.

During the spring of 1992, a Team ID expedition to Ecuador was organised. This involved Tony, Terrence, Jerry, Richard and George. The last two were from the Cambridge group whom we had got to know during the recent years. I couldn't go because we simply did not have the money and because I spent what I did have taking Michael to the recently opened Disneyland in Paris. It also answered the question of an Alpine trip that summer. There would be none, because I had to set my priorities, and at this stage it was family first, climbing second, although I promised myself that I would return to the Alps in 1993.

That summer I experienced climbing from the home front only. Those on the Ecuador trip left in July and came back three weeks later with tales of success on Cotopaxi and Chimborazo. The trickiest moment of the trip had not been in the mountains but when Tony had been stopped by the Columbian police during a stopover and had been taken to a special room for some questioning about his bright yellow climbing boots. Fearing something might be planted on him he insisted on having witnesses.

John and Liz went to the Alps in July too and pulled off a

tour de force. In two weeks, they climbed the Finsteraarhorn, Jungfrau, and the Cresta Rey on Monte Rosa's Dufourspitze along with most of Monte Rosa's summits, before finishing with Mont Blanc and the Dome de Gouter. They had ticked a total of nine 4000m peaks, all done in fast, efficient style with no epics. But they would not be going back. Liz had always had tremendous qualms about climbing in the Alps, where she knew people who had died. This trip was to be a one-off and even though they continued to climb all around the world before they had children, I could never interest them in returning.

The autumn of 1992 arrived and I settled into my new cosy family life. We went to the Dovedale Dash weekend but stayed in a B&B for the first time. In early December, a group of us did a bungee jump in West London. The idea had been Tony's and although I found the experience quite tame after my years skydiving, we thoroughly enjoyed the day with all our wives and girlfriends standing by, commenting and taking the piss. Agata filmed the jumping and as Tony came back after his go, he laughed at the camera and shouted: 'Next time no bungee!'

A week later he went to Spain for a pre-Christmas weekend rock climbing with Terrence, Richard and Bev. I was still pleading a lack of funds and was sitting at home on a Friday evening, playing a game with Michael, when the phone rang. It was Terrence.

'I've got some bad news,' he said. 'Tony's had an accident. He's in an ambulance on his way to hospital.

Can you tell his mother? I can't get through to her.'

'Shit, how bad is it?' I asked.

'It's bad. He's definitely broken his legs and arm. He's got a serious head wound and he's hurt his back.'

'But how the hell? What happened?'

'He was lowering off a climb when his belay gave way. He fell 60ft on to the rocks below.'

'He is going to make it isn't he?'

'I don't know,' said Terrence, 'he's badly hurt.'

This really worried me, but further conversation was brief as Terrence was in a phone box and running out of money. I left a message for Jane, who was out on a works party, to contact me and set off to collect Paul and Sheila. Sheila spoke Spanish and would be able to get through to any hospital. I briefly told them what had happened and together we went to see Tony's mother Nancy, who was at that moment in the midst of a dinner party.

Together we sat trying to ring the hospital that we knew Tony had been taken to. Sheila did a great job and within an hour Tony's mother was talking to a surgeon. Her first question was to the point.

'Doctor, I am a nurse. You can tell me, is he paralysed?'

I could tell from her face that the answer to this crucial question was the right one.

The doctors believed Tony would not be wheel chair bound but they would not yet commit themselves on his chances of survival. With this disturbing news, we returned home.

It took a few days before we learned exactly what had happened and how badly Tony had been injured. Jane decided to fly to Spain to be with him during this difficult time although he remained in intensive care and she could only see him very briefly each day.

Richard rang me to tell me the full story. He and Tony had decided to do a hard route, too hard as it turned out, and after 80ft or so they decided to retreat. Richard had lowered off some tat (an old sling placed a long time previously), which had held. Tony could have abseiled from a peg but he had decided to lower using the same tat. After 20ft the belay had given way, and he had fallen 60ft onto the rocks below. He had not been wearing a helmet and was at the very limit of what was survivable. In fact, I don't think I know anyone else who could have survived such a fall.

Terrence had witnessed the accident and was first to reach him. Tony was conscious with a huge gash in his forehead and with his limbs set at strange angles. Richard, who spoke some Spanish, rushed off down to the road below the crag and flagged down a passing car but even so, it took an hour for an ambulance and stretcher crew to arrive. During this time, Terrence had sat with Tony, gently encouraging him to hold on and all the time expecting he was going to die at any moment.

Once in the ambulance, the other three followed him. He was taken first to the local hospital where the staff immediately decided his injuries were too serious for them to treat, and he was then sent to Seville, another two hours away. The doctors who had looked at him were not optimistic. 'Your friend is very gravely ill,' they told Terrence and Richard.

The following day Richard, Terrence and Bev had come to visit Tony in hospital. They found the bed he had been in empty and stripped. Fearing the worst they approached a nurse, only to find that Tony had been moved to the emergency ward.

A full scan of Tony revealed a horrific list of injuries. He had broken his back in three places, had broken his femur, and had a crushed ankle along with breaks and dislocations of both arms. His skull was shattered, at his forehead and his brain had been visible, which must have been a traumatic sight for Terrence.

This was a huge setback, from which it would take many months, if not years, to recover, but Tony's luck had not completely deserted him. The most eminent back surgeon in Spain happened to be in the hospital. In a major operation, he inserted plates into Tony's back to fix his spinal injuries. This was surgical work, that later brought respect from the British surgeons who were to treat Tony in London.

Several more operations followed in the days after, on his skull and femur, as the surgeons worked their way down the priority list. It took a month before Tony could be moved back to the UK. We visited him in hospital in South London and his ordeal was clear to see. This had been heightened when, on arrival in the UK, surgeons had taken off the plaster, which had been slapped on his crushed ankle. At the time it was put on the doctors had been concentrating on the major injuries and a broken, even crushed ankle, was not a priority. However the ankle had now become infected and for a while they seriously discussed amputation. Fortunately another operation saved his foot.

To say Tony had used up another life would be an understatement. His amazing physical and mental strength had pulled him through this accident and it would prove a turning point in his life. In time, he would recover but his serious rock climbing, skydiving and Alpine 'game' days were over. We would miss Tony in all these activities but these were minor considerations compared to the fact that the most important battle of all had been won. He was still alive. But 'Team ID' would never be the same again.

*'In which Tony discovers that crampons
do have their uses.'*

*'But manages to stop himself just
short of the abyss.'*

5. Discovering the 4000m challenge

Tony remained in hospital for months during which time we visited him regularly. I lost count of the number of operations he underwent, and there was soon little left of his former physique.

'When you recover you'll have to do quite a bit of working out mate.'

'I know, can't wait.'

He bore things incredibly well, and always seemed in good spirits, even planning an expedition to the Himalayas. Then the big day came, when he was allowed home assisted by two crutches. Jane organised a party and we all came round. Gradually he discarded his crutches and started to walk again unassisted.

Tony had been very lucky. He had certainly used another of his lives, maybe two, and we used to discuss how many he might still have left. Surprisingly, within a year, except for a slight limp, there was little immediate evidence of the ordeal he had been through. He could even climb again, as he proved one evening at Mile End climbing wall, but serious running or even regular jogging, were out.

The question of what to do next in the Alps, and with whom, occupied my mind a lot during the spring of 1993. My own dilemma was how to balance family life with more Alpinism. I have to confess this was motivated more by practical than ethical reasons.

Tony's accident had not dampened my own enthusiasm for climbing and I still maintained to myself 'that I would not make the same mistake.' But with Tony recovering slowly and clearly not able to go climbing any time soon, Terrence and I were at a crossroads. Terrence had met a lively, attractive new girlfriend called Joanne, with whom he was spending more and more time and our rock climbing trips had declined dramatically.

My own practical issue was largely solved that summer and incidentally for many subsequent ones, by Agata and Michael's desire for a trip back to Poland to see family and friends every summer. This provided a win-win scenario, which caused no tension between us. I was well aware this was not the case for a number of friends.

The news that dark winter was dominated by the war in Bosnia. The depressing daily reports of massacres and ethnic cleansing made one wonder what had happened to ordinary people in Yugoslavia. It all seemed a long time since the 'end of history' had been announced at the start of the decade.

That spring I talked to the editor of the BBC Blue Peter programme about energy saving light bulbs and they set up a tremendous nationwide competition for kids to design a new light fitting for them, the winning entry of which would actually get manufactured. For several months Blue Peter told the nation's kids about the benefits of saving energy and it gave the whole issue a lot of coverage.

My determination to go back to the Alps in the summer of 1993 was absolute. After two years absence I was really missing a sense of being 'in the Playground of Europe'. But the question remained what to do next. We had climbed the big names, the famous mountains that one's aunt might have heard of. To continue meant researching and learning about mountains which were, to the general public at least, obscure, unknown and uninteresting.

It meant crossing the boundary from climbing things we could tell people about and climbing for the sheer joy of it, without any recognition. I knew I wanted to cross over and no longer felt the need to talk about climbing to outsiders who wouldn't understand. But where, amidst a busy working life, and in a pre-Internet world, could one obtain good information on what the possibilities were? At this stage we still only had the Collomb books for guidance.

It was Terrence who first drew my attention to a significant development. In 1993 Richard Goedeke's new guidebook '4000er Die Normalweg' which was translated, as 'The Alpine 4000m peaks by their classic routes' was first published in English. It was a seminal event in the climbing world and had a similar impact on me as reading 'The White Spider' had had almost ten years previously. Richard Goedeke was a German Alpinist who had managed to capture, in simple terms the magnificence of the Alps. I remember reading with growing excitement the sentiments I felt myself, simply and boldly stated.

'The 4000m peaks are terrific. Quite beautifully big. Quite beautifully cold. Quite beautifully wild' and *'No wonder...so many people collect 4000'ers.'*

Goedeke provided many answers at a stroke. Here at last, was a guidebook for mere mortals, ordinary climbers of 'good average fitness' and not the 'supermen' assumed by the Collomb's guides. I also felt that Goedeke had no hidden agendas, as far as the climbing itself was concerned, by which I mean he was not understating difficulties through cultural conditioning. It was honest, straightforward and realistic reporting. In addition, the guide gave a lot more useful information on where to find the various mountains, the hut climbs with their telephone numbers, simple but clear maps, colour photos and even the dangers and pleasures. It also provided a one-volume overview of the entire Western Alps, and removed the need to accumulate numerous regional guidebooks.

And there was one more important thing about Goedeke. He was environmentally minded at a time when this was not mainstream thinking. I liked his 'green' attitude towards the Alps and the world in general, and this made my commitment to his guidebook, a stronger one.

All these were important and much needed developments but there was one idea, which had an even greater impact. This was idea of collecting 4000m peaks and taking a lifetime to do so. This had not occurred to me before and it suddenly seemed 'the mother of all challenges.'

It meant years, even decades of purpose, providing a rationale for further climbing in the Alps. It also provided a reason I could give to Agata, Michael, my family and the world in general. The 'journey' would be almost as fun as the climbing and there was no hurry. Thanks to Goedeke, we now knew there were sixty-one 4000m peaks. At this stage we were not too concerned whether a top had a height difference of 35m or 20m and the subsequent discussions at the UIAA and elsewhere. Sixty-one was the official figure and that is what I would go for. It was also the final nail in the old imperial measurement system. In 1990 I had still thought of Kilimanjaro as being 19,340 ft high rather than 5895m. From 1993 onwards my thinking was metric.

The whole idea was reinforced by the news that two British guides, Martin Moran and Simon Jenkins were going to attempt to climb all the 4000m peaks in one go during the summer of 1993. Not only this, they would do it in an environmentally friendly way without using any motor transport. This, to us, was so far beyond the bounds of our abilities that it was like reading about a marathon runner breaking the world record.

But we loved the idea and looked forward to hearing how things panned out for them. And, of course, the whole exploit added to the credibility to the 4000m challenge.

Armed with Goedeke I began a study of possibilities and it was, like seeing a painting in its entirety, after years of just seeing small parts. I studied the book for weeks, memorising large sections, as I read late into the night.

The Saas Fee valley seemed appealing to start with. This is adjacent to the Matterdal and Zermatt. It contained a large number of 4000m peaks including the Lagginhorn and the Weismiess. These could both be climbed from the same hut, the Hohaas and I noted that a cable car went all the way to the hut. I was not proud of using railways and lifts, but reasoned that as they existed, they would save time and effort. Our holiday times in the Alps were after all short, and didn't resemble the six to eight week seasons that the pioneers enjoyed.

I consulted with Terrence, who had also acquired the new Goedeke guide and found we were thinking along the same lines.

'Who else could we get to go along?'

'We could ask Richard. What about your outward bound group?'

This last was a reference to a group of outdoor enthusiasts

Terrence had joined in Southampton where he was now living and working. He did indeed put the word out and a guy called Andy answered the call.

Andy was about our age and had some Alpine experience. He was Scottish, easy going and would prove a good companion on the coming trip. His girl friend had no problems with him going either, which always made things easier and less tense. There was one aspect of Andy that Terrence and I would sometimes laugh about. We understood his Scottish accent most of the time, but when he spoke quickly it seemed he was speaking another language. Despite this handicap we met up a few times before the summer, practising a bit of rock climbing here and there.

I also asked Richard Furlong, who at the time had just quit his career in the City. He was going on a trip to South America with John Liz and Jerry. I had also been invited, as had the others, but they were going for too long and I didn't have the money. A week in the Alps was only just affordable. But Richard was willing to do both trips. He would fly back from La Paz and travel straight on to Geneva. This way, he reasoned, it was more than possible that his acclimatisation would be maintained.

I had first met Richard in 1984 and he was part of the CUMC. A good degree from Cambridge was followed by a number of years as a stockbroker in the City. During these years we had occasionally come across each other at various meet ups and events. He was skinny as a rake and consequently a very good rock climber. Nicknamed 'Scummy' for now obscure undergraduate reasons, he was extremely intelligent and, as I would discover, well connected to the New Labour revolution, which was then in its embryonic stage.

We met up once a week at Mile End climbing wall, and after a climbing session, invariably went on to 'Lowfats' house nearby for a drink and a meal. It was during these periods that we discussed climbing, the latest news from the climbing world, and where we planned our own trips. Ideas were bandied about, some absurdly optimistic, some more practical. Richard had a strong climbing record behind him, involving ascents in the

Alps, Africa and South America.

During rock-climbing trip to Mali with Mark and another friend, the three of them had gone for a swim in a local lake. They arrived back in the UK with nine tropical diseases between them and Richard had spent time in a tropical diseases hospital in London. As a result his liver had been affected and he had been advised to avoid alcohol. From that day on he had become teetotal and would not even touch wine. There was a positive aspect of this for the rest of us, which was that buying him drinks was always a low cost option.

Richard had been climbing with Tony during his recent accident in Spain, and unreasonably blamed himself for what had happened. It had preyed on his mind for many months although no one else had agreed with him. He was now planning to retrain as a barrister, which he had decided, was what he really wanted to do in life. One advantage of this was that, suddenly, he had a long period of holiday before starting his training. The plan was, therefore, that Richard would go to Bolivia for a month, then join Andy, Terrence and I three days after we had travelled to the Alps.

Andy, Terrence and I practised rock climbing during some summer weekends at Swanage. Once, we biviied in the entrance of a cave, overlooking the sea. It was peaceful, and certainly removed work stress, but we awoke in the rain and soon beat a retreat to a nearby cafe.

I could only find a precious week to climb that year. With a new family I was lucky to be able to get this. Agata, Michael and I had a week's holiday in Tenerife and they would visit family in Poland whilst I was away. We were also very grateful to my mother-in-law Helena who came to stay with us for long periods helping out with Michael and the housekeeping. She was a very 'easy going' character and gave the lie to the old mother-in-law joke industry. This would establish a pattern for the next few years in which we had a family holiday and then Agata and Michael would visit Poland whilst I was in the Alps.

Three days before our departure date, I came down with flu again. It felt exactly the same as 1990 and I cursed my luck. I was probably as fit as I had ever been due to months of intensive stair training. Now, despite three days in bed, I was still feeling ill when Terrence and Andy arrived to collect me one Thursday evening in early August.

'Christ Nick, you're supposed to be on a mountain within 24 hours from now,' said Terrence.

'I'll be all right in a few days,' was all I could offer.

We arrived in Saas Fee to bright sunshine that Friday afternoon which, in itself, was a relief, as we dreaded a repeat of 1990s poor weather. Saas Fee is situated at the head of the Saastal, a valley that runs parallel to Zermatt's Matterdal, although the two are separated by a huge ridge of 4000m peaks. It is less glamorous than its more famous neighbour but remains an extremely attractive valley in its own right and the view from Saas Fee is stunning. One advantage it has, or at least we thought so, was that it offers fast and easy access to many 4000m peaks. If you only have a week's holiday and the weather is changeable this is not an advantage to be sniffed at.

We visited the local guide's office and discovered that the weather forecast indicated that although the Saturday and Sunday would be good weather, a major depression was forecast after the weekend. We therefore needed to move quickly and this meant foregoing an acclimatisation climb, although we reasoned that a night at the Hohaas Hut at 3030m would certainly benefit us. This is always a dilemma if one only has a week. You have spent months preparing and planning. A week can be both a long and short time in the Alps but I was aware of a huge pressure 'to do something.' It was this feeling that drove me to follow Terrence and Andy to the Hohaas Hut even though I felt far from well.

Our first target was the Lagginhorn, (4010m) which is the most north-easterly 4000er of the Pennine Alps. It is an attractive mountain with two distinct rocky spurs and is primarily a rock peak, usually only lightly dusted with snow. Because of this an early Alpine start is not essential, and the climb involves about a 1000m of ascent with a grade of PD. It was first climbed in 1858 and involved a local Swiss Pastor, his servant, a local guide and four Englishmen. According to

Goedeke, its ascent time from the Hohaas was only 3-4 hours and it had the advantage of being an objectively safe climb.

We set off at about 6.00am and initially made the mistake of traversing too high into the amphitheatre. This meant some exposed rock climbing to get across the rock spur. Once into the amphitheatre, a rising traverse up leftwards took us to the key ridge. There was some grade II scrambling that I would no doubt have enjoyed had I been fit. From the time, however, that I reached the main ridge my strength started to ebb. Despite my fitness I became slower and slower. It became a real struggle to continue and it was clear that my body was still suffering from flu. Stubbornly and stupidly I refused to give up. It was an object lesson in the dangers of summit fever and was not something I would do today. It hurt like hell to keep moving, but something deep inside simply refused to give up. The others remained extremely patient and we remained roped up although this was probably not strictly necessary.

Slowly I forced myself up the slopes, which were easy angled at about 40 degrees. Conditions were good and I felt little sense of exposure. All this helped but it was almost midday before we reached the rather attractive and airy summit. There, I remember sitting down heavily, hugely relieved. I felt no joy, and didn't even take in the view. To make things worse, I managed to crush the end of a finger under a rock, which was only loosely attached to the mountain, and spent the rest of my time on the summit in wrapping a plaster about the bloodied finger end.

Starting down was easier at first, and for a while progress was reasonable. Terrence and Andy remained with me and Andy, in particular, kept encouraging me on. We abseiled down the key rock band on the ridge and from here descended back into the amphitheatre.

It was here I made a mistake. There is a re-ascent of some 200m and half a mile back up to the Hohaas hut. I should have continued downhill to the Weismiess hut and then taken the cable car back up from here. Instead, worried I would be too late for the last ride, I decided to follow the others on the bare scree slopes back up to the Hohaas.

Almost immediately I ground to a halt. Progress could be measured in a few tens of paces, before I would collapse on my walking axe feeling wretchedly tired. Time ceased to have any meaning, and I found myself more tired and exhausted than I had ever felt on a hill before. I was also alone for given that we were now on easy straightforward ground, Terrence and Andy had moved on ahead.

I found myself playing mind games, setting myself small intermediate targets such as a rock or a level of elevation. Never has so relatively short a distance seemed so far. I was going at the pace of someone on crutches and each step felt as draining as if I was carrying a rucksack full of rocks. Several times I collapsed and had to wait a few minutes before I could summon up the strength to continue. It took me two and a half hours to re-ascend those 200m.

Finally I reached the Hohaas and sat out on the veranda with the others simply relieved my ordeal was over. 'Sorry chaps, I guess I may have to miss doing the Weismiess tomorrow.' I knew I had been stupid and shouldn't have been out that day, and felt no pride in what I had done or even in the colossal effort it had cost me. There was no pleasure at all, a day I wanted to forget as soon as possible. But something, deep inside of me refused to let go. Some spark of this stubborn instinct remained for after a short nights rest, I awoke at 3.00am with the others and announced I intended to climb the Weismiess (4023m). At this stage my mind had definitely disconnected from my body in some way.

Thinking I had somehow recovered I received an enthusiastic response from Andy, or as close as you can come to enthusiasm when waking for an early Alpine start. Terrence was more sceptical. After breakfast we set off and moved towards the glacier. Within minutes I was slowing and in trouble again. At the start of the glacier Terrence made the obvious decision for me.

'Look Nick, you can't go on like this, I'm not climbing with you right now. It isn't a question of your ability. We all know you can climb this mountain but today you're simply not well enough.'

This reasoned argument suddenly hit home and I finally, reluctantly, decided to give up. I returned to the hut, collected my sleeping bag and went off to bivi by the edge of the glacier. I simply needed to be as close to the mountain as possible.

The lads, unencumbered by my presence were back by 10.00am having climbed the Weismiess, only some 13m higher than the Lagginhorn. We descended to the valley and found a local campsite. In general I have always felt the valley near Saas Grund deserves a better quality campsite than it has, but that afternoon I was too tired to care.

The weather forecast had been accurate. After two days of clear skies and sunshine, we awoke to low cloud and drizzle on the Monday morning. That evening we were due to meet Richard at Brig station. We spent the afternoon studying the Aletch Glacier from Bettmeralp where we had taken a cable car. Terrence had wanted to take a closer look at the Aletschhorn, which he wanted to climb one day.

Richard arrived on time and we were quietly amazed by his appearance. His naturally skinny frame had just undergone a month of weight loss in Bolivia. He looked like Ghandi on a bad day, and I have never seen a more improbable looking Alpinist. That evening, we listened to his stories from the Andes. How Richard and Jerry had climbed a local 5000m peak and how Jerry and Liz had got within 30m below the summit of Huyana Potosi (6088m.)

He laughed as he told the story of how he and John had spent a day driving towards Sajama, one of the world's largest volcanoes and near the border with Chile, before John suddenly remembered he had left their tent in a taxi, back in La Paz. They had no choice but to return to the Bolivian capital, itself at 4000m. Despite this they had finished in fine style, by climbing Illimani, (6434m). None of these climbs were guided, and Richard was so enthusiastic about the places, that I made a mental note for the future.

The weather the next morning was still bad, so we decided to travel to the Italian lakes, some three hours away, for a rest. Here we spent two days, waiting for a break in the weather, and during this time I finally recovered from my flu.

Thursday afternoon we returned to Saas Fee. Our objective was the Alphubel (4206m.) The Eastern flank is a 1330m long snow plod across a glacier with numerous crevasses and I remember we chose it in anticipation of poor weather.

The Alphubel is a mountain of many faces and had been first climbed back in 1860 by Leslie Stephen who would later become the father of Virginia Wolf. This had been during the golden age of Alpinism and Leslie Stephen himself would later write 'The Playground of Europe' about his Alpine climbing experiences, which was a title we would quote a lot at the time.

Before we went up to the Langflue from where the climb itself would start we had a huge pasta meal in Saas Fee. I topped this with a gigantic 'Coupe Denmark', an ice cream that represented more calories than Richard had eaten in the past two weeks. On arrival at the Langflue we found that another dinner was included in the cost, and because of this we forced a steak down for good measure.

At 4.00am the following morning the weather still looked ominous. In the distance we could see lightning strikes in the Oberland, and there was thick cloud ahead of us. Despite this, we decided to set off and see. After four days of waiting, and a record number of calories, we were steaming with energy.

Now fully recovered from my flu, I led off through the glacier, jumping across crevasses here and there, and going around others. After a short while, a shout came from down the rope. Andy had fallen into a crevasse up to his waist, but he was soon out and we continued.

A pale dawn slowly appeared, and only one other party from the hut joined us. We alternated the lead, and after the glacier was passed, worked our way up the Alphubel's long easy angled slopes. As we approached the summit we found ourselves in a whiteout with a strong wind blowing. The top of the Alphubel is a flattish plateau where, in good weather, one could play a game of five-a-side football. We groped our way across this plateau, with visibility down to five meters, before deciding we had reached the highest point. This was determined on no other basis than that the other party, led by a guide, had also stopped there.

The climb had taken four hours fifty minutes and we had no summit view. It was the first time I had been on an Alpine summit in these conditions, and I was pleased to realise my clothing and equipment were up to the challenge.

Three hours later we were back at the Langflue, pretty pleased with our efforts. We stopped to talk with the other party that had climbed the Alphubel that day. The climbers turned out to be Germans, who were also climbing and collecting 4000m peaks. I remember them speaking with excitement and passion about a recent ascent of the Bishorn, and I recalled Goedeke's statement:

'No wonder...Many people collect 4000ers'.

We swapped stories of routes and places and it felt good to be with fellow travellers, total strangers, who shared the same passion and vision.

This was the final climb of the trip as we had run out of time. In many ways the week should have felt unsatisfactory. A stupid flu ridden ascent, followed by another snow plod in total white out conditions, was all it was. Yet it did not feel like that. The magic of being in the Alps made these points seem trifling. I had been again to that special world of snow and ice, which was so difficult to explain to those back home who remained sceptical of what we were doing.

It had been a fairly gentle re-introduction to the Alps, without much risk and I certainly felt few ethical concerns at this stage about such climbing. With Agata and Michael happy with their own holiday there was no reason why this should not be the first of many more such trips. I knew that outsiders did not understand but I simply shrugged this thought off. After a break of a couple of years my desire to climb was stronger than ever. Little did I know, but 'the game' would never be so harmless again.

*'The Coup Denmark was the size of
a small mountain.'*

6. New Team ID

Something had happened to Terrence after Tony's accident. Despite climbing three 4000m peaks during the summer of 1993, it became more and more obvious that his heart was no longer in the game.

The first hints had come after his ascent of the Weismiess, when he had stated that he was no longer interested in snow plods. During the autumn of 1993 and spring of 1994, he became more and more involved with Joanne, and although she encouraged him to go climbing as often as he liked, his interest was clearly waning. He was still willing to go rock climbing in the UK and expressed an interest in visiting the Dolomites but he would not commit himself to the Alps for the summer of 1994.

Maybe it was because I was not present when it happened, but Tony's accident did not cause me to closely question the risks involved in Alpinism. Despite having a new family, and a young son, I was still comfortable with the thought that I was not taking any real risks. I would quote statistics about road deaths to defend my own Alpine climbing as reasonable. I had confidence in my abilities and judgements and was determined to continue.

This meant that I found myself looking for new friends to go to the Alps with. It was about early March when I got talking to a colleague at work in the canteen. John Rothery or JR as we would get to know him, was telling me about a recent solo trip to the lakes, where he had biviied out under the stars.

'Just to get away from it all.'

As this had happened in winter I took notice and suggested that John might like to join us at Easter in North Wales for a weekend's climbing.

For the same trip to Wales I had invited another work contact, a journalist called James Hunt who had just been to the Karakorum mountains of Northern Pakistan. James and I had been rock climbing for a day at Chepstow the previous summer and had got on well. He was extremely enthusiastic about climbing and willing to have a go at almost anything.

During the Mile End evenings, I had already persuaded Jerry to join us too. Now a veteran of Africa and South America he was keen for some new adventures.

It was agreed that the four of us would travel together to Snowdonia where we would meet Terrence. At the last minute my younger brother Will also joined the party. Will, who was ten years younger than myself was about to take his finals at Lancaster University. His heart was made of pure gold but he was lacking in what might be called 'common sense'.

It was cold, dark and wet when we arrived in Snowdonia on the Thursday night before Easter. Terrence was waiting stoically outside the local pub and we were just in time for last orders. As we left I discovered Will had not brought a jacket or any sort of waterproof coat. It had simply not occurred to him that this might be essential.

'I've got a few spare jumpers with me.' he said confidently.

We sorted him out with a spare jacket, but the incident allowed us, as a group, to break the ice and we had a very pleasant weekend's hill walking. We got on pretty well as a team and, as we chatted and walked together, I learned more about my new companions.

JR was a tough Geordie from one of the toughest parts of Newcastle. His working class background had left him self-sufficient whilst his intelligence had got him to university and beyond that to postgraduate work. He had been extremely fit in his youth and had once cycled from Newcastle by himself to the South of France on a budget so meagre it did not include anything for overnight stops or even enough food. He had slept by roadsides, in fields and ditches during his six-week trip, and he had even eaten raw vegetables he had picked up from fields on the way.

This youthful fitness however had then been largely negated, by a decade of sloth and alcohol, as he started a career in the electrical industry and came into money for the first time in his life. At this stage, he was re-evaluating his life and was attracted to the idea of getting fit and doing something challenging.

One of the striking aspects of JR was his extreme rationality, his ability to analyse something dispassionately and logically, coupled with an encyclopaedic knowledge of almost any subject you could care to mention. He now lived in South London where he had recently bought a flat. His strong ethics were reflected in the fact that he was a strict vegetarian.

James Hunt was older than the rest of us and came from Brighton where he lived with his wife Zoe and young daughter Mia. He edited a number of technical magazines and had spent many years involved in motorcycle racing. This had slowly been curtailed by rising costs but not before he had experienced a number of near misses. His enthusiasm for anything to do with the mountains however was manifest and infective. He was also a keen environmentalist. James was willing to try any walk, climb or scramble that came his way and he was also as I would discover very fond of beer. He was the only one of us with Himalayan experience, and his easy-going nature and sense of humour would stand us in good stead in the future.

Jerry Baum, on the other hand, was more of a red wine man. He amused us with tales of his dating experiences within the North London Jewish community, where he was always looking for a girlfriend. Each week he would set up a new date, and although sometimes things would progress to a few follow up dates, there was always something not quite right. During the winter months at the Mile End climbing wall he would inform us of some recent disaster or amusing incident, always with a grin and good humour. He was working at Imperial College, and lived in North London in a three-bedroom flat, which he had wisely bought during the late 1980s.

It was this 1994 Easter weekend in North Wales, which saw the start of a New Team ID. Inadvertently, I had stumbled on a new team of blokes who were compatible, congenial, and all inspired by the idea of Alpinism, before they had even experienced it. The four of us came from different backgrounds, held different views on many things, but on this one central issue of climbing the 4000m peaks, we were as one.

The only thing at this stage that we lacked was joint Alpine experience, and we knew the only way to acquire it, was by going to the Alps in the summer of 1994. We were also in total agreement on the fact that we would not be using guides. This was not due to any lack of respect for this magnificent profession, but rather because we felt it would diminish the challenge, in letting others make our decisions for us. We instinctively rebelled against this idea, preferring to make our own mistakes, and trust in our own abilities, and judgements to get out of trouble. The satisfaction of climbing a mountain this way was also greater.

The world seemed a sad place at the time. The seemingly endless Bosnian war was still dragging on, with its depressing daily news bulletins. My army cousin had been sent there on an unpublicised mission, and had returned with a shrapnel wound. I reflected that after a generation of peace, he had experienced three wars in his six years since joining up - the third being Northern Ireland. Clearly a job in the army no longer meant decades of cold war training, but involvement in the real thing.

It was also during this period that I first experienced the Internet. It was incredibly slow but my IT manager told me that it would be a lot faster in the future.

From that time on we met regularly at the Mile End climbing wall where we made our plans for the summer. In fact these would prove quite complicated, as we had a number of variables. Terrence, JR and I would travel to the Dolomites for a week's rock climbing in August. After this week, Terrence would return home whilst James and Jerry, who could only take one week's holiday, would meet JR and me in Zermatt campsite. Then, at the last minute it was also agreed that Richard Furlong, alias Scummy, and Alec Erskine would join us for the two weeks although we would climb as separate parties.

We drove to Cortina in mid-August 1994 arriving in that amazing world of vertical spires and huge rock faces. Once again, three days before we left, and after months of training on the stairs, I came down with flu. I began to suspect this was not a coincidence but something psychosomatic, linked to some form of subconscious stress. It certainly wasn't conscious and I was upset at yet again starting a trip feeling ill.

The Dolomites were awesome - not a word I would use lightly. All around us were towering limestone spires, so much larger and higher than anything on offer in the UK. Here the game was not about steady, safe climbing with good protection, but instead, it involved the art of moving fast and trusting to ability and experience. Above all, the Dolomites were intimidating.

We had an easy first day up at the Cinque Torri, a well-known group of rock towers near Cortina, which offer short rock routes of up to 140m. We climbed the South East face of the Torre Inglese graded IV-, which took a few hours, after which we had some beers in the sun at a local cafe. That evening we moved up to the Dibona hut near the Tofana di Rozes.

We had just moved into this pleasant wooden hut when Richard and Alec arrived. The following day we set off to climb a 'Via Ferrata', on the Tofana di Rozes. This started in a cave, and we soon became aware we were now climbing along the Italian World War One front line with Austria. Evidence of old fortifications was all around, and I subsequently took a great interest in reading the guide book descriptions of battles from the period, and the remarkable effort it took just to stay alive in this area.

Half way up the route I suddenly began to feel unwell, and retreated to the nearby Cantore Hut, for a cup of tea.

Terrence and JR continued to the summit of Tofana di Rozes before joining me at the hut for a drink. We were soon joined by Alec and Richard, who had just climbed the 800m South Face, graded IV-. They were smiling, but it had been a major effort, and they had clearly been stretched.

The following day Terrence, JR and I climbed the South West face of the Torre Grande. Graded IV this route was 140m, and it took us three pitches to get to the summit. Here we had a tremendous view of the surrounding area. On descent, however, we abseiled down the other side, and soon got off route. We ended up descending a steep scree slope, down a natural tunnel, before coming to a final abseil. At this final point there was a bolt, with bit of bright red tat, which we gratefully used.

A few months later I described our descent to Paul 'Low Fat', knowing he had been to the Dolomites just before us, and mentioned the tat. He smiled and said.

'That was my tat. I did exactly the same thing a few weeks before you.'

'That's amazing, so you got off route too?'

'Yeah, it wasn't clear at all.'

After staying in huts for the first three nights we now found a decent campsite near Cortina itself, which served some of the finest pizzas I have ever eaten. It was from here we set out later that week for a day out at the famous Tre Cime di Lavaredo, also known as the Drei Zinnen. This refers to three vertical rock pinnacles each as large as the Eiffel Tower.

Terrence, JR and I chose the South West Face of the Cima Piccola - the smallest of the three towers, but still more than 300m of climbing, and graded III.

'What does the guide book say?'

'It's not very detailed, a few paragraphs only.'

'Christ, is that all? This route is over 300m.'

'Let's give it a go, maybe it's obvious.'

The route wasn't obvious, and the short guidebook description was all we had for the 300m ahead. I think we were on route for maybe the first two pitches, after which things became vague. The rock was poor and quite often we kicked rocks off the edge. After reaching a major ledge we gave up on the guidebook, and decided to find our own route up the face. The rock improved but there were no bolts, or signs of previous parties having come our way. This was where our UK climbing experience came into its own, as we pitched and protected our way up the rock face.

After four hours and about 12 pitches of mostly comfortable grade III or V Diff standard, we came to a small ledge. There was a huge peg, which was the first sign we had seen for hours that others might ever have come this way. This was the crux; not of our route, but some major desperate face route about six grades harder than what we had been doing.

We were about 30m below the summit of the Cima Piccolo, and the exposure was the most extreme I have ever experienced. Not only were we looking straight down 280m to the start of the climb, but we were also aware of a further 1000m void to the valley floor below that.

The way ahead meant making a non-reversible traverse above this exposure, with a fall meaning a major swing out onto the face if the peg held, or a 1280m plunge for all of us if it did not. Nor could we see what was on the other side of this traverse, and the climbing was probably grade V or HVS. It's important to know where your limits are in climbing, at least for 'ordinary Joes' like us, and after a few half-hearted attempts, we jointly decided this was indeed what we had just reached.

Getting down was not easy. Terrence tied our two 9mm ropes together and I started setting up an abseil.

'I didn't see any pegs on the way up,' I said, 'we're going to leave a lot of gear behind.'

'Yeah, and most of it's going to be my gear and slings,' observed Terrence.

'We'll all pay to replace them,' said JR.

At this stage, I think all of us would have paid quite a lot of money, if someone could have spirited us back to the cafe at the bottom.

I recall we had to do twelve double rope abseils. We set up belays with slings around rocks, or wires in cracks. It was nerve-wracking work, but the rope only jammed once as we pulled it down.

'I'll go up and clear it,' I volunteered.

'You're not going to be able to tie on though, the route up is on the left and the rope is stuck on the right.'

I ended up soloing half way up the pitch in order to free the rope.

On one occasion I remember that the rock around which we had set up our belay, moving, as JR put his weight on it at the start of another abseil. We were calm and collected but the tension was always there, just under the surface. We could not avoid knocking off rocks, which went crashing into the gully below and into an area where we knew Richard, and Alec had started their route. This added an enormous feeling of guilt each time it happened, and I dreaded killing someone below with a rock I had kicked off.

It was dusk, when we regained the path down to the cafe and our car. As we walked back, lost in our own thoughts, we met up with Alec and Richard who had just completed the West Face of the Cima Grande. They too, were in reflective mood, and I sensed a mild state of shock as they described hours of hanging belays and exposure whilst climbing near their limits.

I felt tremendous respect for those pioneers who had first conquered these routes. As an experienced skydiver I was not normally worried by drops but can state with confidence that the exposure, and the frightening nature of the climbing on these great Dolomite cliffs, is the key factor which needs to be overcome when climbing here.

Once we were safe, though, our collective sense of humour soon returned.

'At one stage I decided as I wasn't going to be needed for anything for the next 20 minutes I'd stick my head in a crack to avoid the exposure,' was JR's comment!

'I think we were on the correct route for about one sentence of the guide book.'

'I've never spent so long in rock boots. My feet are bloody well misshapen.'

After this there was an unspoken need to change gear for a few days, and we spent the last days doing Via Ferratas, with pleasant stops at cafes in small Dolomite villages. Our last evening was spent in the campsite bar, where we had another great pizza and spent a memorable evening discussing philosophy, science and the problem of induction. We finally agreed this was an insoluble issue.

I am convinced that it is really important to have some idea of where your climbing limits are. It is the search for this limit that eventually kills so many top climbers, as was evidenced by the huge casualty rate amongst top British and continental climbers at this time. I myself had briefly been caught up in this dangerous cycle in the mid 1980s, where success at one level necessitates an even harder, more dangerous route next time.

My own cycle had been broken when I fell and broke my ankle - an event that confronted me with this reality. However, many people don't stop and push themselves across some invisible line. I suspect they know well what they are caught up in, but are unable to break free from it. It could be peer pressure, commercial pressure, or some inexplicable internal drive, but whatever the reason, if nothing comes along to break the cycle, it often ends in death or serious injury.

We left the Dolomites knowing that we had reached our rock climbing limits. I no longer had a desire to risk exploring the world beyond. Even on the right side of my limit, I would find plenty of challenges.

We dropped Terrence off at Brig station, from where he would take the train to Geneva and a flight home. I was conscious at the time, as I saw him go, that this might be the end of an era and, although we could not be sure, it was indeed to prove Terrence's last climbing trip to the Alps. We would continue to do other things in the UK, and in time, become godfathers to each other's daughters, but our serious climbing days together were over. In many ways Terrence is the most normal guy amongst my climbing friends with a strong, practical approach to climbing. I would miss his presence.

Another thought also crossed my mind, as we saw Terrence off. What if we rushed up to Tasch and caught the last train up to Zermatt? We could bag the Breithorn the next morning, and be back by lunchtime to greet James and Jerry at the campsite, as planned. So this is just what we did, racing up the Breithorn standard route from the Kleine Matterhorn in an hour and ten minutes to enjoy a fine view. It was JR's first 4000m peak, and even allowing for its easy nature, we were well pleased with our efforts.

We just had time to take up relaxed postures in the Zermatt campsite, when James and Jerry arrived. We soon moved on to a local bar to plan the next few days. After some discussion we decided to have a go at Pollux (4092m) and Castor (4228m) the next day. The weather forecast was good for another day, after which it was set to worsen. This would be the first 'New Team ID' Alpine climb.

We caught the first cable car up to the Kleine Matterhorn and set out confidently along the Verragletscher glacier below the Breithorn Ridge. We crossed a serious crevasse zone and approached the early slopes of Castor. It was at this stage that Jerry decided he wasn't acclimatised and fit enough to continue.

'You guys go on I'll wait here.'

'You sure Jerry? Do you want to rest for a bit before going on?'

'No, it's all right. I'll lie down in my bivi bag.'

We agreed to leave Jerry near the Zwillingsjoch where he could see us for the rest of the route and we started up the South West Face of Castor. The going was straightforward, although we could sense that in different conditions the slopes we were crossing would be avalanche swept.

It all got tricky towards the top left, where the slopes connect to the summit ridge. Hard ice, and suddenly steeper terrain, meant we had to be cautious and at some stages we were front pointing in order to stay attached to the slope.

The summit ridge was exposed enough to make us concentrate on our feet, to make sure that we didn't trip over our crampons. We reached the top of Castor in variable cloud, and consequently got only an occasional view or sense of our surroundings. The summit itself was small and reasonably exposed, but there was nobody else present and we felt pleased with ourselves. It was James' first 4000m peak, and I filmed him with my video camera, although we were all lost for words.

A Briton, along with his Swiss guides, had first climbed Castor in 1861. It is the higher of the so-called 'Zwillinge' (twins) alongside its companion peak, known as Pollux.

It had been our intention to climb Pollux after Castor but, although we had summited within guidebook time, it was now clear we would not have time to do this - at least, not if we wanted to be on the last cable car down from the Kleine Matterhorn. This was some six kilometres of soft snow, and 250m height gain away.

Having made this decision we made our way back down the summit ridge and the slopes below to be met by a most amusing sight. Sitting in the snow in his bivi bag was Jerry. He had zipped the whole thing up, except for a few inches, through which he was conducting a conversation with two women climbers, who had just knocked on his 'bivi bag door' to check he was OK. Jerry, who looked like a gigantic caterpillar on the snow, was clearly enjoying this unexpected female company, and was oblivious to our return.

We mercilessly 'took the piss,' at this turn of events, which Jerry took in good spirits despite the fact he must have been disappointed not to reach his first Alpine summit. It is, perhaps, a comment on our lack of fanaticism that we all preferred Castor and an evening in the North Wall Bar and no Pollux, rather than Castor, Pollux and a cold bivi, or a long epic descent in the dark.

As we returned we spotted a tent along the route, flapping in the wind. Its owners, we reasoned, were doubtless somewhere climbing above, and we didn't pay it more than a fleeting glance. Our return became a race against the clock as we needed many stops and the re-ascent of some 250m was taxing after a long day. The distances along this glacier are deceptive and in soft snow it actually took longer than the journey out.

In the end we made the last cable car with five minutes to spare, and had our night out in the North Wall Bar after all. Richard and Alec, who had stayed in the Dolomites to do another route, joined us later that evening. They had plans to climb the Weisshorn, and the next morning they disappeared down the valley, for the hut climb.

This was the day we also met up with my friend Marcus, another journalist, who had arranged to join us in Zermatt. He wanted to do a few climbs but was also planning to write an article on the rescue services in Zermatt. We had decided to have a rest day after Castor, and spent the day relaxing in

Zermatt, seeing Whymper's broken rope in the museum, reading guide books in shops, that sort of thing.

Late that afternoon Marcus joined us for a beer. He had just interviewed the head of mountain rescue services in Zermatt and was full of information.

'So how was it?'

'Very interesting. The guy is sick and tired of picking dead bodies of mountains.'

'Not surprising.'

'How often does he have to do it?'

'He says this week it's already seven - that's more people than have been reported dead in the siege of Sarajevo during the same time. Only yesterday they collected a guy who had been camping up near Castor. Apparently he went out for a pee in the middle of the night and was struck by lightning. He was killed.'

'So that was the tent we passed up there.'

'Apparently his mate, who raised the alarm, had to be rescued too.'

'What does he think is to blame for most accidents?'

'He says inexperienced people, with no gear. He showed me a slide cabinet full of photos of bodies. Apparently they always photograph the bodies.'

'Christ, what was it like?'

'Horrible. He asked me to take some of the photos and publish them, anything to shock people into an awareness of the risks out here.'

'And did you?'

'No chance - my newspaper would never publish them.'

That evening we decided to have a go at the Allalinhorn in the Saastal. This was chosen due to the fact that it was described as easy, would suit Marcus, and that changeable weather had been forecast. Goedeke described the Allalinhorn (4025m) as *'an easy proposition'* and I noticed that a joint Anglo-Swiss party had first climbed it in 1857.

The following day was both memorable and farcical. Despite the fact that I have never refused to use mechanical transport to get to mountain huts, climbing the Allalinhorn from

Zermatt in a day felt uncomfortable. We took an early train to Tasch, and then drove round to Saas Fee, from where we took a cable car and mountain train to the MittelAllalin station (3500m). All this took two hours. We kitted up and started on the 580m climb, which was graded F, and which only became interesting above the Feejoch. The final slopes were hard ice, and we needed to take some care, but after two hours we reached the top.

The weather had been cloudy and changeable, and did not allow more than a few glimpses from the summit. The top point itself is adorned by a cross and necessitates a few metres of rock scrambling, and a queue had formed to stand next to the summit cross. It was here we had an altercation with an old local guide, who suddenly tried to push his way through us to the front.

We were a friendly, civilised bunch even under pressure but there was something so objectionable about this action, so un-British, that we formed a line to prevent the guide from forcing his way past us. The coup de grace was JR thrusting his face in front of the guide, and staring him down.

Later we heard more stories about local guides from fellow campers. One of them actually had her belay suddenly unclipped by a guide, who came up to switch it over for his own rope. Such an action could have had serious consequences. Once again, these incidents all seemed to involve older guides, not the younger generation, but they illustrated a clear territorial sense and a frustration with our presence. No doubt they would like to have banned all non-guided climbers from the area.

We took our summit photos and congratulated Jerry and Marcus on their first 4000m peaks. In truth it all felt rather easy, but I would still recommend the Allalinhorn for anyone interested in making his or her first 4000m ascent. Goedeke might still have added '*but it remains a nice day out.*'

The farcical part of the day occurred back at the revolving MittelAllalin restaurant. We arrived to hear that the mountain railway, which had brought us up here, had a fault and was not running. How long the repairs would take no one knew, but management had been authorised to offer us all free drinks whilst we waited. This turned into a significant drinking session as the Swiss Alps slowly revolved around us. It was a strange experience to have on an Alpine climbing holiday, especially as we were reacquainted with our 'parked' rucksacks once an hour!

Some hours later we descended to Saas Fee, and were still in high spirits by the time we reached Zermatt. This was just as well for the weather had finally broken. Anyone who has spent some time in Zermatt will know how it can rain. We sprinted to the North Wall bar and did not leave until closing time. Richard and Alec joined us too; flush from having climbed the Weisshorn.

'How was it guys?'

'A bloody long way, but excellent climbing.'

'It was a bit of an epic really.'

The rain continued to fall all of Wednesday, and the weather forecast predicted even worse for the rest of the week. So by Thursday morning, when indeed the rain did get worse, we decided to bail out and visit the Eindhoven Jazz Festival in the Netherlands where my parents lived. It was the end of August and Zermatt had a very 'end of season' feeling, which I found quite depressing - as if the deck chairs were metaphorically being stored away. I determined there and then, never to go to the Alps that late in the season again.

It had been a fun few weeks, and we had laughed a lot. As a team we had developed together well, and agreed to return to 'the game' the following summer. Our next trip would belie the idea that we were in total control of our destiny in the mountains. But that all seemed a long way in the future, and we envied the young English couple we had met in Zermatt campsite who were taking a few years off in a campervan, to climb around Europe. They would be heading for the South of France whilst we would be returning to work.

'In which Jerry deployed his 'chat them up en route' ploy.'

7. Scaring Brother Will

One day at work, I had a call from our reception to say that someone claiming to be my brother was asking after me. I went down to collect Will, who looked exhausted and clearly hadn't been out of his clothes for a week. Over a coffee he explained he had just returned from a solo mission to deliver a rucksack full of vitamin tablets to a Croatian refugee camp. These camps were a direct result of the Civil War in former Yugoslavia, and the sad news from this part of Europe still dominated our TV screens.

Will, moved beyond endurance, had decided to take action. He had spent most of his grant on Vitamin tablets, and had then hitchhiked to Zagreb, sleeping rough on the way in midwinter. I couldn't help but be impressed with his compassion and commitment, but then noticed his rucksack still seemed to be full.

'So what happened once you got to Zagreb?' I asked.

'I was caught up in a storm just outside Zagreb. I sat in the snow with only my poncho to cover me and I've never been so cold in my life,' he said. 'Next day I went to the British consulate in Zagreb but it was closed.'

'Hmm, shame,' I commiserated. 'So what did you do then?'

'Well I decided to hitch hike home as I couldn't find any refugee camps.'

I looked in his rucksack, and found it still full of vitamin tablets.

'But why couldn't you just give them in somewhere else? You didn't have to hand them in direct at a refugee camp, did you?'

'I didn't want to give them to just anyone,' he answered.

'So let me get this straight,' I said. 'You just hitchhiked to Zagreb in midwinter to deliver a rucksack full of vitamin tablets to a refugee camp but, because our consulate was shut and you couldn't find a refugee camp, you decided to bring them all the way back to London?'

'Yes.'

'Jeeesusss, Will.'

This incident summed up my brother. He was full of idealism, generous to a fault, and willing to undergo tremendous hardships to reach a goal. All this however was undermined by the fact that he was still missing a 'common sense' gene. As I watched him drinking his coffee, an interesting thought suddenly crossed my mind. If Will could be persuaded to come on an Alps trip, he might be willing to carry all the heavy stuff, as he was very fit and strong. Team ID might be able to move faster than it usually did.

Will had graduated from Lancaster University in the summer of 1994, but a lack of funds and the need to find a job had meant he was unable to join us in the Dolomites and Alps in 1994, something, which with hindsight was just as well. By 1995 he had both a job and funds, and was keen to join us for a trip to the Alps that summer. This meant I suddenly felt a new responsibility. Not to bring Will back in one piece would be unthinkable, and I decided to try and make his introduction to Alpinism a good one.

During Easter 1995, New Team ID spent a long weekend rock climbing in Derbyshire. We decided to 'practice our prussiking', which is a key way of getting out of a crevasse, by climbing the rope, although I had never actually met anyone who had done it this way. In order to simulate the real thing, we rigged up a rope on an overhanging cliff and hung about practicing. Will had borrowed Tony's bright yellow fluorescent plastic boots, which glinted in the sun and stood out for miles around. We had a lot of fun, laughed a lot and attracted a good deal of attention. That night in the pub we were highly amused to hear our neighbours talking about their day.

'Did you see those prats hanging around on their ropes?'

'Yeah, one of them was wearing bright yellow boots, and didn't seem to know his arse from his elbow.'

'God, what was that all about?'

This was the time when 'New Labour', under a youthful Tony Blair, was making progress in the opinion polls, helped by a Tory party, which seemed determined on suicide. It was also during the spring of 1995 that I read Joe Simpson's 'This Game of Ghosts'. Like many others, I had read and enjoyed his first book 'Touching the Void' a few years earlier but I found 'This Game of Ghosts' a more powerful book. Simpson was my generation, and I knew several of the people mentioned in his book. But it was the essence of being trapped on a moving escalator, of always looking for something harder next, and being unable to stop - even though knowing your luck was likely to run out at some point - which was for me the most powerful subtext of the book.

A tragic number of Simpson's friends and contempories died in this way. They were good climbers whose luck just ran out. In fact during the 1980s and early 1990s an entire generation of leading British climbers was decimated, and it was only due to several miracles that Simpson himself was not amongst them. I found the book a fascinating insight into the psyche of top-level mountaineering.

We had only one precious week to spend in the Alps that summer. There was a consensus that after our rain-affected visit the previous summer; it should not be spent in Zermatt. Goedeke had already opened our eyes to the possibilities of the Bernese Oberland.

'You know it's not just about the Eiger there. How about the Mönch or the Jungfrau?'

'Yeah. We could stay at this Mönch Hut.'

'You get there by taking a train ride through the Eiger. They even stop to let you look out down the North Face.'

This last fact swung it.

Mindful of his appearance in Wales a year before without any kind of waterproof clothing, I made sure that Will had all the gear he needed before we set out. He borrowed plastic boots and a jacket from Tony, and the rest of us found enough gear between us to complete his kit. I then also forced him to take out BMC - British Mountaineering Council - insurance.

JR, Will and I drove to Grindelwald in late July. It was the time of the Srebrenica massacre in Bosnia when the French President wanted to send troops to take back the enclave from the Serbs, whilst the then British Prime Minister John Major had vetoed the idea. Emotions were running high and I strongly suspect this was the reason why a French truck driver, on seeing our English number plates, tried to drive us off the road at 5.00am. With no one else around, he made several obviously deliberate attempts, which fortunately JR was alert too. This was still mostly a pre-mobile phone world, and there was little we could do at the time.

In Grindelwald we met up with James and Jerry. It was stiflingly hot, 42 °C, and there was a good forecast for days to come. Once again, after months of stair training, I had come down with flu three days before setting off. By now I was convinced that this was subconsciously stress-related. Fortunately I would have a rest day first, because although we had decided to go straight up to the Mönch Hut, we would spend a day acclimatising, and practising our snow and ice work before attempting a route.

We took the Jungfraujoch railway and enjoyed views of the Eiger North Face as we made our way for the first time to the top of the railway. The route up to the Mönch Hut is a straightforward hour's walk across a glacier, and we'd got half way when we were caught in an unexpected summer storm. Lightning lit the sky and we witnessed several strikes nearby, which caused our ice axes to hum. Suddenly there was a large flash only a few hundred yards away, which certainly got our attention. Then, just as we were about to leave our metal gear in a pile by the side of the track, the storm cleared almost as quickly as it had appeared, and we caught our first view of the overhanging frame of the Mönch Hut.

As we arrived I saw Will with a big smile on his face.

'Well, the beer should taste good up here,' he said.

'What beer?'

'I've brought a six pack up as a surprise for you all.'

Behind the counter at the Mönch Hut was a stunningly attractive Swiss girl, who spoke perfect English. Jerry was particularly taken with her, and would always offer to get anything from the hut counter, something that kept us all constantly amused.

The following day was all sun and blue skies, and after the climbers had disappeared off on their routes, we found ourselves alone, and in the way of the hut staff, for whom this was an opportunity to clean up. The Swiss girl asked us with a smile why we were not 'Climbin ze Mönch', in a way that seemed to question what kind of men we were.

But we stuck to our plan for a rest day, and spent the afternoon practising our crampon techniques, doing snow brakes and also reconnoitring the first part of the Mönch South East Ridge.

That evening I sat in the warmth of the hut, watching Will try and get rid of his cans of beer. He managed to get JR and James interested, but I was still feeling the after effects of my flu and Jerry didn't drink beer.

'What are we climbing again tomorrow?' asked Will.

'It's called the Mönch,' I replied. The guide book says it's OK except for the summit ridge, which is supposed to be quite exposed.'

'Hmmm,' was Will's answer.

'Don't worry you'll be fine, just don't look down when you're on it.'

The Mönch (4099m) had first been climbed in 1857, during the golden period of Alpinism, by an Austrian and two Swiss guides. In 1952 John Hunt's British Everest team had also climbed it in winter, as preparation for their triumph of the following year. Goedeke described the South East Ridge as '*a short but very attractive climb*' and this we would soon attest to.

The following morning we set off early. The lower slopes were verglassed, but straightforward, and the ridge part was very pleasant, with scrambling similar in standard to Striding Edge on Helvelyn. Being fit, we set a fine pace and soon reached the snow ridge just before the summit ridge proper. James led up a steepening slope, which in those days had not yet been equipped with stanchions for protection. Every now and then I would look behind to see the others following and even Will looked relaxed, although his rucksack looked heavier than ours.

The summit ridge lived up to its reputation, being both very narrow and quite stunningly steep on both sides. This is not a route for people who cannot handle exposure. We worked our way steadily along, trying not to think about the drop either side of us. It really was a case of the old saying - 'If you fall into Switzerland, I'll jump into Italy.' On this ridge, if one person fell off one side, the second would have to jump off the other to balance the fall!

The weather remained superb and we had the summit to ourselves. I got out the video camera and filmed everyone and then sat down to enjoy, what I considered then and still do today, the finest view in all the Alps. You can see the Matterhorn in the distance and the Eiger close up. It is this contrast, which in the clear air and the sparkling white and rocky landscape around makes it so special.

It had been a great effort by Will, whose first 4000m peak this was, and I slapped him on the back and told him so. He smiled, and then completely spoiled the moment by asking me if I'd like a can of beer to celebrate with. Yes, he had brought his cans with him. This time he found no takers and we smiled when, after attempting to open one himself, he found the beer had frozen in the can.

After a while, a Dutch husband and wife team, who were ticking summits in the area, joined us. Will and I had a brief chat with them in Dutch, and I remembered hearing that they had found the Jungfrau a bit tricky.

But mostly we just sat in silence struck by the view, munching on chocolate bars and all the time knowing we had to descend the exposed arête that we had just come up. It is this knowledge that prevents the Mönch summit experience being completely relaxing and enjoyable.

We must have spent at least half an hour on the summit, which from my experience was a long time, but the descent was not far, and we had plenty of time. Partly we were also in no hurry to face the exposed ridge again, and these factors combined to allow us the kind of summit experience I had always dreamed of but rarely experienced. In the end though, we steeled ourselves, and set off down.

As Whymper's party had done with the young Douglas Hadow on the Matterhorn in 1865, we placed the inexperienced Will in second place behind James, with JR mentoring him from the middle of the rope. Jerry followed him with me bringing up the rear. I had decided to film the ridge as we moved along, doing this by jamming the camera between my arm and body whilst still holding my axe and the rope in front. Despite never once looking through the viewfinder I was later pleased with the way the video came out.

Will was fine along the summit ridge, but once he reached the steep snow slopes on the upper part of the ridge he began to run into problems. The exposure suddenly began to take a grip, and he found himself struggling to descend the softening snow. He was given a crash lesson in how to lean back on his crampons, and we continued our descent, but it was a turning point for Will. It was as if his mind had finally caught up with what his body was doing. As a result, our progress down was slower than it had been the other way.

We stopped frequently to admire the views, and allowed ourselves to smile more, as the worst of the tension disappeared. With all these stops and rests it was mid-afternoon before we arrived back at the bottom of the climb. Our spirits were high.

'Another one ticked off.'

'Damned good effort, Will!'

'I wouldn't like to do that summit ridge again.'

We were preparing for the ten-minute walk back to the Mönch Hut when Will turned round, and without a hint of irony asked:

'Which one have we just climbed?' The walk back to the hut was a light-hearted one after that.

That evening, the others, having not yet reconciled themselves to the expense of hut food, cooked outside the hut, using their little Tranja stoves. It has to be said, the levels of competence varied.

Knowing that James was not a natural cook, his wife Zoe had given him some simple boil-in-the-bag meals. For some reason he had managed to cut a number of holes in one of these bags, and he ended up with a bowl of chilli con carne soup!

JR and Jerry on the other hand were more capable chefs, and both being vegetarians had decided to join culinary forces for the duration. They produced a fine platter of Noche with vegetables, which looked and smelled good. Will and I simply ate the hut dinner.

That evening, the key decisions were made about the next day. JR, James and Will would set off at 4.00am to climb either the Gross Fiescherhorn (4049m) or Hinter Fiescherhorn (4025m), depending on how they felt. I was still feeling the residual effects of my flu, and decided to have another rest day so as to be ready for the second half of the week. Jerry also decided to duck out of this one. His motives were less clear, and he was mercilessly ribbed for wanting a longer chance to chat up the Swiss girl.

The lads were off at the appointed hour, and Jerry and I had the luxury of a lie in. By mid-morning we had breakfasted and Jerry was sitting on the hut's veranda chatting to the Swiss girl. Time dragged for me, and by early afternoon I decided to go out on to the Ewigschneefeld Glacier to see if I could spot anything. At one stage a helicopter flew by, and I remember starting to feel worried. What if something had happened to Will and I had not been there?

One by one the parties that had set out that morning for the Gross Fiescherhorn returned up the glacier. None of them seemed to know anything about our trio. By now I had wandered about 500m down the glacier, and time was moving on. Three o'clock became four o'clock and there was still no sign of the others. Then, just as I was starting to get seriously worried, another party of four came up the glacier. This team turned out to be four British women who had just climbed the Gross Fiescherhorn, and they reported having seen three English guys descending the slopes back to the glacier above them. This allayed my fears somewhat and shortly after three figures did indeed come into view way off down the glacier.

Distances on glaciers are always difficult to estimate and it took the figures more than two hours to get close. By now I could confirm it was JR, James and Will and was more relaxed about things.

As they reached me I could see they had had a major epic. James looked seriously ill, whilst Will was staring wildly, sucking a prussic loop and giving monosyllabic answers to any questions. Only JR was coherent.

'Have you brought any water with you?' He asked me.

'Sorry, I didn't think I was going to be out this long.'

Will then asked if he could go ahead, and shot off up the final slopes towards the hut. Whatever was wrong, it wasn't his fitness. James looked completely wrecked, worse than I had ever seen him, and even after I took his rucksack we advanced slowly.

During the climb back up to the Mönch Hut, JR talked about what had happened. They had set off at a good pace, and had reached the bottom of the glacier slope between the two Fiescherhorn summits in guidebook time. However, their subsequent ascent of this face had been slow and James had started vomiting soon after. Instead of turning back, they had slowly worked their way up the very icy face to the summit ridge of the Gross Fiescherhorn. This was a long, exposed ridge, which demanded care and took time. Four-fifths of the way along this ridge Will had ground to a halt. He simply didn't want to go on or back alone, and as they were only a hundred metres from the summit, JR had lashed him on to the ridge itself.

'You'll be OK here Will. Which way do you want to face?'

'Towards the summit, looking towards the way you're going,' said Will.

'OK, we'll be back soon.'

So JR and James had left Will trussed to a rock on this exposed ridge, whilst they continued to the summit of the Gross Fiescherhorn (4049m). Will had watched them, petrified they would fall from the ridge, and leave him alone. His worries, however, proved to be unfounded and within an hour they were back. James was still being sick, and they had used up their remaining water trying to rehydrate him.

Their descent of the steep gullies that led to the snow slopes was painfully slow, as the ice was rotten and the rocks loose.

Finally, after a draining effort they had emerged on to the snow slopes above the glacier. After a while they decided to bum-slide down these slopes, and had careered down wildly. Will had gone into James' back with his crampons, which hadn't helped.

Once down on the glacier they faced an exhausting three kilometre walk and 350m climb back up to the hut. They were suffering badly from dehydration and Will, having decided this time to leave his beers at the hut, found comfort in sucking his prussic loops. It was soon after this I had seen them.

It was getting dark before we managed to reach the hut. It had taken 16 hours to do the round trip and we had had to support James up the last bit. He continued to throw up in the hut itself, and was soon lying comatose in his bunk. It was only afterwards that I realised I had stood waiting on the glacier for more than seven hours.

We were now out of synch. Jerry and I felt fit enough to do another route the next day, but there was no question of the others joining us. We therefore decided to descend to Grindelwald for a rest.

We arrived back at the Kleine Scheidegg to see our Swiss girl waving to Jerry. She was about to cycle back down the valley to Interlaken for a short break, after which she would cycle back up, ready for another shift at the Mönch Hut. We were seriously impressed.

In the campsite it was 40°C and this, combined with our piles of clothes, socks and boots, meant our fellow campers gave us a wide birth. We decided not to go back for the Jungfrau. The comments by the Dutch couple, combined with the fact that after four nights in the Mönch Hut it was difficult to face going back, led us to consider alternatives.

'Where can we go and get two more routes in before the end of the week?'

'Not Zermatt!'

'What about Chamonix?'

'No let's go to Saas Fee. We could do the Lagginhorn and the Weismiess.'

This last was my suggestion as it offered a chance to return to some unfinished business. The others quickly agreed and we drove around the Grimsel Pass to Saas Grund. Before we took the chair lift up to the Hohaas Hut, we went to hire some crampons for Will. He made his decision purely on cost.

'What's the cheapest pair you have?' he asked the guy in the shop.

A pair of crampons was subsequently produced which looked as though they had last seen action in the 1930s. Will was sold at first sight.

'Will, for Christ sake, you need to get a decent pair. It's a false economy.'

'Rubbish, these are fine,' he said confidently, as if he had half a lifetime's experience behind him.

It was pointless to argue, and Will walked out with his choice nicely wrapped up in a bag, and a highly amused shop owner, smiling in his wake.

The Hohaas (3100m) hadn't changed since I had last been there two years before, and we were soon settled in. I persuaded everyone to have a go at the Weismiess first, rather than the Lagginhorn, using the arguments that it was the higher of the two and that arguably on a clear day you might see Milan Cathedral from the summit, this last being a quote from Goedeke.

The Weismiess (4023m) is the highest mountain in the North Eastern Pennine Alps, east of the Saas valley. It is also described as the most beautiful, with a major ice and snow face on one side and gneiss rock faces on the other. It was first climbed in 1856, and unusually for the period, there were no Brits in the party. We were determined to do the North West Face which is graded PD, and is described as having '*Impressive glacier scenery and in good visibility a fantastic panorama view'*.

I knew from experience that there was a rather nasty crevassed glacier at the start of the route. We crossed this without incident in the dark, and it all seemed so easy I wondered whether it was the same mountain that I had seen a few years earlier. There were only a few other parties out that day and we would have most of the route to ourselves. Daylight came, and we were soon plodding up the 40-degree snow slopes towards the summit ridge.

Half way up there was a cry from Will.

We were well spread out on the rope, and it was hard for me to see what was happening.

'What's up with Will?'

'His crampon's broken,' came the reply

'Surprise, surprise!'

We mercilessly took the piss, and placed Will in the middle of the rope. It has to be said he managed well enough despite this handicap, and after three and a half hours we emerged onto the squalid summit. The snow all around us was stained yellow, as if an entire rugby team had relieved itself after a night out on the town. Even more disappointing was our inability, despite the good weather, to even see Milan let alone its Cathedral.

'I want my money back,' said JR disappointed.

As there was little incentive to linger and no one felt like sitting down on the summit, we slowly descended the steep summit ridge. A few hours later we approached the glacier at the start of the route. Now in daylight, it looked very different from the place we had passed in the dark just a few hours earlier.

'I don't believe this is the way we came up.'

'Shit, this looks nasty.'

'Let's be really careful.'

'Prussik loops at the ready everyone.'

We were clearly off the route we had ascended earlier that morning, and life became more and more worrying. We found ourselves jumping across numerous smaller crevasses and were surrounded by much bigger ones. Most were clearly visible but we knew this could change at any moment.

As I looked round I could see serious concern etched on all our faces, except for James, who was leading and really enjoying things. He would cross a crevasse and stop to look back down before moving on to adopt a protective position. I was just suggesting to James that he might start doing this more quickly, when I felt myself falling through the snow. Fortunately I jammed at the waist and after a bit of swearing pulled myself free. I looked back at Will. He did not look happy and I could only imagine his thoughts. It was one of the nastiest glaciers I have ever been on and we were very relieved to reach the edge by the path down to the hut.

Back at the hut we enjoyed the usual beers and banter but Will seemed in an odd mood. It was as if he had crossed some invisible line, and when the conversation turned to the Lagginhorn (4010m) he was strangely reticent. Then one by one people started to drop out. James reminded us he had promised to visit some friends who lived near Lake Geneva and headed off. Shortly after, Will declared he wouldn't be climbing the next day either, as he didn't feel like it any more. I tried half heartedly to persuade him without success. Jerry too was uncertain, and then declined. His fitness was not yet good enough, he said, for two routes in two days.

The next morning, JR and I woke up and got ready. I went to the bathroom and discovered I had some serious conjunctivitis and squeezed a good deal of pus out of the corner of my left eye. As I put my contact lenses in it crossed my mind that maybe I shouldn't be climbing a 4000m peak in my current condition, but after a quick consultation with JR I decided I couldn't let him down. At breakfast we had a chat with some French women who were setting off before us to climb the Lagginhorn.

'We're just going to take it easy,' we said. 'Maybe see you up there.'

'Alright, if we're going, we'll go light,' I said. 'No rope or video camera and only a water bottle and chocolates.'

JR agreed and we set off just before dawn.

We moved quickly as we were fit, acclimatised and carrying little. I used my knowledge of the route to lead us round and up into the amphitheatre and we were soon heading towards the West Ridge proper. About 50 other climbers had set off before us and gradually we started to overtake them.

Once on the ridge, and above the rock band, we struck perfect conditions. It was here I suddenly felt as if I was Popeye after knocking back the spinach. For the first time I was able to make full use of the months of stair climbing without having to wait on a rope.

My pace fastened and I hit a steady rhythm. Even JR who was normally the strongest in our party, started to fall back. I raced past dozens of climbers, literally running up until I reached the front of the line of climbers.

Leading the way were a German couple, who were clearly intent on being the first to reach the summit. As I started to close in on them, they started to speed up. Accepting the challenge I went into overdrive, pushing an internal turbo button. Within minutes I had put a demoralising 50 feet between us, and the race was over. I had never felt this strong on a mountain before, and it was a sheer pleasure to climb that morning, rather like jogging without any pain. I mention it because it was the only time I was ever to feel this on an Alpine route.

I reached the top alone, far ahead of anyone else. It was a fantastic feeling to sit alone on that rocky summit, and enjoy a view, which was both expansive and inspiring.

I spent a deeply satisfying ten minutes before the German couple joined me, and we then had an odd but pleasant chat about the merits of the Channel Tunnel, as opposed to the ferry. Having just had a bad experience with the Tunnel, I argued in favour of the ferries, whilst they preferred the new high tech trains. It was a surreal conversation to be having in the circumstances and it ended after ten minutes when JR joined us.

We laughed at ourselves and shook hands in very British fashion. It was the only time I have been on an Alpine summit without a camera and it didn't matter. It was all such a massive contrast to my previous ascent of the Lagginhorn in 1993.

Soon the small summit began to fill up and we decided to set off down. A few hundred metres down the ridge we came across the French girls we had seen at breakfast.

'We thought you were going to take it easy,' they called out.

JR and I looked at each other, and then both said at the same time.

'But we did!'

The girls laughed and moved on. Back at the hut Will and Jerry had barely woken up, when we ran back in.

It was Friday morning and the end of our climbing for the week. JR had climbed four new 4000m peaks in six days whilst

James, Will and I had climbed three. Jerry was happy with his brace and we celebrated in the bar in Saas Grund that evening.

Will seemed relieved it was all over. He had experienced a traumatic week, for someone who, as I had now learned, was scared of heights. It had started with him almost being struck by lightning and a scary, exposed ascent of the Mönch. This had been followed by an epic on the Gross Fiescherhorn, during which time he had spent an hour lashed to an exposed ridge, wondering what he would do if James and JR didn't return. Then he had been forced to cross a crevasse-ridden glacier in softening snow, expecting to fall through a hidden trap door at any moment.

All this, and I hadn't even asked him to carry any of the heavy stuff, not even a bottle of mouthwash!

Will had certainly had a hard introduction to the 'game', something I had not intended and which left me feeling guilty. The main thing, however, was that he was still in one piece and didn't seem to blame me for what had happened.

But it would be nine long years before he agreed to go back to the Alps to climb with us again.

'So which way do you want to face Will?'

Eiger summit 1984 – for some reason I had taken my hitchhiking board with me.

Just above the clouds. Eiger summit at 4.30pm.

1987, just before our Matterhorn attempt. Tony left, Terrence centre, Author right. – Note the rudimentary gear.

1988 - Eating a tin of corned beef on the summit of Mont Blanc was my most impressive achievement that day.

1989 - A priest blesses us all at the Hornli Hut. Any help at this stage was welcome.

1989 – Success looks and feels like this. L-R Tony, Author, and Terrence on the summit of the Matterhorn.

1990 – Mark, Tony, Terrence and author on the early buttresses of the Eiger. Note the improvement in gear since 1987.

*1990 - Tony and the author in the Jeckyl bar Chamonix
celebrating Tony's survival.*

*New Team ID 1994 – Marcus, Alec, JR, Richard, Jerry, author
in the North Wall Bar Zermatt.*

*1994 - JR about to start the first of twelve double rope abseils
on the Cima Piccolo.*

*1994 – Jerry's bivi en route ploy with James and JR looking on.
The girls had already moved on by this stage.*

8. A dangerous game

If the summer of 1995 had its tricky moments, the summer of 1996 saw Alpinism become a dangerous 'game' for New Team ID. It was also the first time that I began to have some doubts about what we were doing. None of this was apparent, though, during the winter of 1995/1996, when I continued to dream of new climbs above the snowline.

Somebody showed me Will McLewen's book 'In Monte Viso's horizon' which describes his own journey to complete all the 4000m peaks, along with advice on many aspects of climbing. McLewen was clearly a very good climber, far above my standard, but it was his chapter on bivouacking, which really caught my imagination. Until then, a bivi - for us - had been something to avoid at all costs, something you might not even survive. McLewen, not only put this fallacy to rest, but also showed that a planned bivi could be a life enhancing experience.

I determined to put these ideas into practice, and acquired a Gore-tex bivi bag for the purpose. The first opportunity was somewhat amusing. Terrence and I drove up to the Lake District, and ended up biviing on a damp night in a lay-by off the A6, with lorries thundering by a few feet away. It was January and there was still some snow and ice on the ground too, but to my amazement I spent a thoroughly comfortable night. From then on, I slept out quite often, even when tents and houses were available. It was a tremendous confidence boost to know that ordinary climbers like me did not need to fear a night out, even high in the Alps.

The first May Bank Holiday of 1996 saw us continue a tradition, which had started a few years before. Together with wives and girl friends, we travelled to Normandy for a weekend's rock climbing or canoeing. Typically, we would rent a gite and have the run of the place. That year, we stayed in an old church at L'Onlaye l'Abbee. It was squalid even by our standards. Then, on the final morning, we were woken by a class of school kids traipsing through our dormitory, on their way to their classroom next door. There was a lot of sniggering from both parties.

Life was looking up. In London house prices had started to rise, although we were still in negative equity after six years. The economy was recovering after the recession of the early 1990s, and we now had a company car from Philips. Each Thursday night we would meet in the curry house after climbing at the Mile End wall and talk about our lives, the news in general, and future plans. This was also the summer of Euro 96 and football was 'coming home'. Philips was a sponsor and I managed to get to see a few games at Wembley, and even met the then England captain David Platt. I watched the England versus Germany penalty shoot out from a caravan park in Scotland with Agata and Michael, and I was struck by the delight on young Scots faces when England were knocked out.

Tony and Jane now had a one year old son called Thomas, who provided us with an insight into what it was like to take babies on trips like this. Tony had recovered from his injuries to such an extent that he was now actively planning a trip to the Himalayas, 'to climb something big'.

That winter, I started to put on weight for the first time. My training for the summer was not as thorough as it had been in previous years, and I found it harder to go the extra mile. Jerry on the other hand was getting stronger, and James and JR seemed stronger than ever. In 1996, for the first time, I would be the slowest member of the team. None of this meant my enthusiasm for the Alps was waning, but everything was going to get a lot tougher.

Another book caught my attention around this time. 'Alps 4000', was Martin Moran's story of his epic 52 days traverse, with Simon Jenkins, of all the Alpine 4000m peaks. I had known of this awesome achievement since 1993, of course, but now read the details for the first time. It was a feat so far beyond my imagination that it seemed hard to relate to at first, but when broken down into component parts, it was truly inspiring. Moran and Jenkins would do things in days, which would take us weeks to even attempt, but each part of what they had done was recognisable. I had by now climbed enough 4000m peaks to be able to relate directly to parts of their story.

We decided to go to the Alps for two weeks, and would start in Alagna with the Italian side of Monte Rosa. This was new territory and promised to offer a large number of 4000m peaks in a short period.

There was also another reason we were heading for Italy. This was the year that the scandal broke about the Swiss banks stealing Jewish gold, which had been deposited during or just before World War II. Subsequent Swiss governments had lied to the world about what had happened, and it was only after a Swiss bank employee, who had been ordered to destroy evidence, had sent it to the US instead, that the truth was revealed. Even though the Swiss government had agreed to pay compensation after a US threat to derail the Swiss economy, we felt our own protest was required. We would not be visiting Switzerland in 1996.

Richard and Alec would join new Team ID again and it would be a repeat of the summer of 1994, in which we would climb separately but drink together. We arrived in Alagna after a long night's drive and set up camp in its pleasant surroundings. I have a fondness for these Italian valleys, which seem so much quieter and peaceful than their counterparts on the other side of the Alps. There is one other factor, which is that - for me - Italian food is so much better than Swiss and the prices are generally far cheaper.

Richard and Alec arrived that evening and we had a great Pizza at a local hostelry. I was planning to make a film of the climbing trip, and after a good deal of wine we had jokingly assigned ourselves characters from the Whymper story. Alec and Richard were the Taugwalders father and son, whilst JR was Hadow and Jerry the reverent Hudson. I was Croz and James, for some reason I cannot remember, became Reinhold Messner.

The next day we all took the cable car to Punta Indren and made our way up to the Gnifetti hut. The route to the hut involved scrambling up an unexpected rock step, which added some fun to what we had expected to be just a slog. The Gnifetti

Hut (3647m) offered a chance for some acclimatisation and I remember it being a rather large but pleasant hut.

We had a good weather forecast and the excitement of being back amongst the Alps was palpable. But getting up for an Alpine start was just as hard as ever, and none of us were very bright at 4.00am the following morning. The initial slopes up towards the Balmenhorn were straightforward although we did spot some crevasses lurking in the shadows beyond our head torches.

After a few hours we reached the Balmenhorn (4167m) with its small wooden hut and huge statue of Jesus Christ on top. This was where we planned to spend the night. Technically this was a 4000m peak. Goedeke, despite being scathing about its status, had still included it in his lists although in reality it was little more than a small rock pinnacle sticking out of the snow. We, however, were not complaining and were happy to claim another summit. Deciding to leave our heavy sacks at the hut, we set off for the Vincent Piramide (4215m) and the Corno Nero (4322m.)

By now I was suffering from altitude sickness for the first time in my life. We plodded up the Vincent Pyramide in less than an hour, and I had to sit down on the summit, unable to enjoy the occasion. The others were smiling, shaking hands and full of banter whilst I felt wretched.

Despite this, I was determined to continue on to the Corno Nero, also known as the Schwarzhorn by the Germanic world, and this turned out to be by far the most interesting summit we reached that day. The approach was straightforward but then the final part was steep, or rather very steep. I estimated it to be close to 60 degrees and once we had negotiated this we arrived on a summit ridge, which was narrow and very exposed. On one side was the slope we had just come up, whilst on the other side was about a kilometre of freefall.

Even with a headache and nausea, it was impressive, and cameras were passed back and forth as we all clung to the razor sharp ridge. After a few minutes we started to descend, and all I could think of was my feet and my head. The world around me didn't exist even though the view was tremendous, and the situation we were in, exciting. I was second on the rope behind

James as we front pointed downwards facing in.

Suddenly, I heard a scuffling noise and glanced up, to catch sight of JR cartwheeling down the slope. He was literally tumbling head-over-heels and I remember jamming my axe in, and waiting for the force to hit me and pluck me off the mountain. But the strain never came, and it took me a few moments to realise that Jerry who was between us had held the fall. Not only that, but he also had a wound in his thigh, as JR's crampons had glanced off him. Our reactions were immediate.

'Well done Jerry.'

'Bloody well done old man.'

'So the Reverend Hudson held Hadow's fall this time!'

Our gratitude was sincere. It was true that the slope had a run out, but still we would have gone a long way down had Jerry not held, because I know I would never have held the two of them. Jerry's wound turned out to be a small crampon scratch to his left thigh - a very close call in all senses, and we returned very much chastened to the Balmenhorn Hut.

We arrived there to find it deserted. Goedeke had described it as squalid, but we found it rather pleasant as if after a makeover. It was clean, had a table and chairs and enough bunk space for ten or twelve people. We were able to make tea, and I slowly started to feel better. An hour or so later Alec and Richard arrived. They had just climbed the South Face of the Vincent Pyramide, and had experienced a bit of an epic. This was not due to the difficulty of the climbing, but because of the fact that a sharp edge had almost cut right through their rope whilst they were on a hanging belay.

'I just watched the rope unravelling before my eyes,' said Alec

'Here's the rope,' added Richard who held up a mostly severed bit of 9mm cord.

Despite this our spirits were high. We were tired but content with our day's work. Our yarns were well embellished and provided the main evening entertainment. Three 4000m summits in a day was a new experience, even if one of them was the much abused Balmenhorn.

Then, shortly after dark, the small hut started to fill up with

Czechs who had appeared, apparently from nowhere. About 17 of them came in and the small sleeping area in the loft suddenly became seriously overcrowded. There was just enough space for a person to lie on his side, whilst he or she was wedged in between two others. Given that the ceiling was literally only inches from one's head, and that the hut began to overheat and smell badly, it became a real trial of character.

James was worst off, as his Czechs, an aging mother and her middle-aged son, were both semi naked and pressed up against him. Getting up was impossible, without half a dozen other people moving first. So we spent the night like sardines, overheating in sleeping bags and praying that our bladders would not play up. Slowly, very slowly, dawn arrived, and our human pile began to unpeel itself.

It's fair to say we were not feeling at our best in the morning, and the weather had broken with a thick cloud cover limiting visibility. It was also snowing lightly. The four of us were desperate to get going, anywhere, just to get away from the Czechs. Richard and Alec, perhaps more used to squalor, wisely decided to wait for the weather to clear.

Our objective for the day was to get to the Margherita Hut on top of the Signalkuppe (4556m) the highest hut in the Alps. As visibility was non-existent there was a premium on compass and map. JR supplied the first, and reminded me that I had been asked to bring the second.

'So, let's have it then.'

I dug in my rucksack and produced my Goedeke guide and turning to the correct page, proffered the book's map.

'Christ, is that it?'

The map was about two inches-square and showed parts of three sovereign countries. Arguably one could make out the suburbs of Milan.

'It's all right. We can just follow the trail up. It's either that or breakfast with team Czech Republic.'

This last point was the most convincing argument in the circumstances, so we roped up and set off into the white-out.

For a while all went well. The trail headed in the right direction and we made steady progress. Then, after an hour, the trail split - one line went up and the other horizontally. After some more interpretation of the two square inches, the decision was made to go up. It was the wrong decision.

The trail got steeper and steeper, and before long we were traversing along a 40 degree slope. The weather was still bad with little visibility so it was impossible to see where the slope ended. At this stage a couple of climbers who had been following us decided they would take over the lead. We all said good morning, and they passed us carrying heavy looking sacks with the Austrian flag clearly displayed.

We were now about 10m or so behind the Austrians, on a slope that had steepened to 45 degrees, and was becoming icy. Suddenly the second Austrian slipped and started sliding down. Within seconds, if that, he had picked up enough speed to pull his companion off the face too. One of them screamed as they fell down into the misty void and disappeared from view.

'NOBODY MOVE,' shouted JR.

I felt dazed. Had we just watched two guys die in front of us? It had happened so quickly, and I was struck by the ease with which the first guy had pulled the second one off the face. For a few seconds we neither moved nor spoke.

'It's a bit icy up ahead.' James was looking along to where the Austrians had fallen.

'We should go down the slope and see if we can help them.'

'Yes we've got to try, but let's be bloody careful.'

Although unattractive, this seemed morally the only decision we could make, and cautiously we started front pointing down the slope. After 15 minutes of this, the cloud cover suddenly started lifting, revealing a nasty, steepening slope below, and then some 200m further down, the two Austrians. One was in the Alpine emergency help position; the other was lying in the snow. It was clear one or both was in serious trouble. We waved in recognition and encouragement, and kept on heading down.

After half an hour, we had descended perhaps 50m and the slope began to get steeper still. It was already 50 degrees and getting worse, when James, who was leading down, shouted up that things looked even steeper below that.

'Let's stop for a moment,' said JR.

'I think we should go back up,' I said. It felt bad not to be able to help the Austrians but we had to put our own safety first.

Then a group of climbers appeared below and started attending to the Austrians. Spotting us, they began to shout and wave. It turned out we were perched a few hundred feet above a monster crevasse that would have fitted two London buses side by side. The Austrians must have cleared it in freefall. If any of us slipped now we would be unlikely to be so lucky. The only positive was that James alone could see the crevasse.

We concluded a short meeting, spread out as we were on the 50-degree slope. The consensus was to reverse our route entirely, and for the next half hour we front pointed upwards on a mixture of hard snow and ice. There was no real protection; a slip by anyone would probably have meant everyone coming off. Stupidly, we felt confident enough not to bother stopping to put in some ice screws, but we did indeed prove that when it really mattered, we could climb. Adherence to the face was literally by the front points of our crampons and the picks of our ice axes, which were smashed into the ice.

Slowly and deliberately we worked our way back up to the level where the Austrians had fallen. JR decided that he would cut steps back to the easier ground, a few meters away, and we all watched transfixed for the next ten minutes, as he set to work with his ice axe. He succeeded in sculpting the M6 in 45-degree ice, after which we shuffled along back to where the trail became less steep.

An hour later, we were back on the correct lower path and passed the spot where the Austrians had landed. There was still a group of guides standing around, but it was impossible to tell what had happened to the Austrians.

We did not hang about, as matters were clearly in hand, and from here it took us a few hours to climb up to the Margherita Hut. Here we found that Alec and Richard had arrived a couple of hours earlier and were now out bagging some local peaks. On the way up we had witnessed two more guides racing down from the hut with a stretcher, presumably for the Austrians. I regret to say we never did find out what had happened to them.

It took some time to unwind at the hut from the tension of the ice slope. We did some comfort eating, drank soft drinks with lots of sugar, and analysed what had happened and where we had gone wrong. We had set out in a whiteout unsure of where we heading. We had branched off from the correct route even though we were only ever a few hundred metres from the right path. As a result we had not realised we were traversing a steep ice face, rather than the easy, well-trodden path below. A proper map would have helped, as would have some well-placed ice screws on the steep slope.

Because of the circumstances of our arrival, we had not really focussed on the fact that the Margherita Hut is, in fact, on the top of the fifth highest mountain in the Alps. Indeed, it was our fourth summit of the trip so far. The bedrooms upstairs were surreal. I lay on my bunk bed looking out of a window and down on the Liskamm.

'God look at this. Count the 4000m peaks.'

'This has got to be the best view I've ever had from a bed.'

'You've had a sad life then mate.'

At the hut we met a British guy who lived in Belgium, where he had qualified as a guide. His mate was suffering from altitude sickness, and was planning to descend before first light. Richard and Alec also set of before first light, to climb the Cresta Rey route on the Dufourspitze.

We were up a little later, at about 6.00am, when we witnessed a lovely dawn rising above the Alps. The view consisted of subtle hints and tints, rather than deep full colours. It was as if an artist had painted his canvass with only very thin pale watercolours. I remember thinking that there was nothing else on earth I would rather be doing and witnessing at this particular moment.

It took us 30 minutes to cross from the Margherita to the summit of the Zumsteinspitze, which at 4563m is the fourth highest summit in the Alps. Only the last few feet offered any climbing that required any thought but we were rewarded by another stunning view, which included the frontier ridge across to the summit of the Dufourspitze, which I had climbed seven years earlier.

We sat for some time in silence, still drowsy from lack of sleep, and lost in our own thoughts. After a while I did some filming and James and our new friend considered climbing the ridge across to the Dufourspitze. There was a problem however, as we only had one rope between us all and none of the rest of us fancied the ridge. As James didn't like the idea of soloing the ridge, there was little need for further discussion.

We continued to work our way down and across the massif to climb the Parrotspitze (4436m), which was graded PD and the Ludwigshowe (4341m), which rated a mere F. Both were straightforward and we were finished with them by mid morning. There were no further incidents and we decided to descend back to the valley.

That afternoon back at the campsite, we were joined by Richard and Alec, flush from success on the Cresta Rey. After much needed showers we had a fairly riotous evening.

We had been lucky at times, but the four days we had been away had been some of the most enjoyable I had yet experienced. The Italian side of the Monte Rosa massif has much to commend it. It allows quick access to a large number of 4000m peaks, and offers a different style of valley floor. As we left the following morning, I made a mental note that the Italian side of the Alps was worth exploring further.

Mindful of our commitment not to visit Switzerland, we drove across Northern Italy and round to the Mont Blanc tunnel with Chamonix as our destination. It was our first visit as New Team ID and the lads were keen to see the Jeckyl and Hyde Bar I had talked about. We camped at the Molliasses, finding a place against the hill side and walked into town.

Chamonix, unlike Zermatt, has few grassy meadows of note. The tree line dominates the sides of the valleys and starts low down. The mountains and rock pinnacles appear steeper and more jagged than elsewhere, and the Boissons Glacier, though in steady retreat, is still one of the dominating features. And above it all rise the domed peaks of Dome du Gouter, Mont Maudit (Mont Maudit is only a dome from Chamonix – it's actually very pointed!) and the monarch itself, Mont Blanc.

I had read an article that summer about a traverse of the Midi-Plan Ridge in which a young woman related her own first Alpine experience. She and some friends completed the traverse, but were benighted on their return and forced into an unplanned bivi. I had smiled at this last point, but was fascinated by the route itself. Although there were no 4000m summits, it was a classic Alpine traverse and a good introduction to the range.

That evening I suggested the route to the others and after some questions they all agreed. The route followed the ridge from the Aiguille du Midi across to the Aiguille du Plan, after which we had a choice of descending the Envers du Plan Glacier and the Mer de Glace, or returning via the same ridge.

The following day however the weather was poor and we ended up drinking lots of beer in the newly renamed Jeckyl Bar. A young couple were now running the bar who knew nothing of the past, but it was recognisably the same place that I had spent time with Mal Duff six years before. We needed most of the next day to recover and prepared for a dawn start.

'Should I take my bivi bag?' asked James, who had just splashed out £90 on a new one.

'I wouldn't bother,' I said, 'there's little chance of a bivi, and anyway I have a survival bag with me.'

'Hmmm, OK.'

Next morning we caught the first cable car up to the Aiguille du Midi (3812m). From here we kitted up at the famous ice cave and set out down the exposed ridge. This ridge was like a sobering wake-up call, as the exposure is immediate and threatening. It is made worse by the suddenness in which you are propelled from a nice comfy cable car environment to a tight ridge, all without any time to warm up.

The weather was perfect and we continued along a number of even more exposed snow ridges. It was not difficult terrain, but required steadiness of both foot and nerve. After a while we climbed a steep snow face and emerged onto a snow plateau. The panoramic viewpoint was a good introduction to the Mont Blanc massif, with its spread from Mont Blanc round to the two Rochefort summits and further round still to the Aiguille Verte.

One thing was evident. The summits in this part of the Alps appeared far more jagged and steep than the Matterdal.

After a while, we reached a rock ridge, which petered out to a large abseil point. Looking over the edge, it was clear that our single rope was not going to reach the top of the glacier below. We were slow, actually very slow. I abseiled halfway down to a ledge, but before the others joined me an approach had been made to some French guides, who had a double rope rigged up, to ask if they could use these. Surprisingly this had been allowed, and we all quickly availed ourselves of the opportunity.

From the bottom of the rock face a snow plod led up to the Aiguille du Plan. We decided to forego the last part and descend the Envers du Plan Glacier. Had we known what the conditions were below we would have returned the way we had come.

In the midday sun the snow had softened and our descent started to slow. We met some Brits coming up the slope and they warned us that we would soon be coming to a massive bergshrund, with a narrow snow bridge across it. They looked relieved to have left it behind. Shortly after this meeting the ice started to get steeper, and the crevasses become more frequent and wider.

After an hour of this we came to the monster bergshrund. I had never seen anything like it, a huge chasm with a small, unsupported snow-bridge across the top. It was wide enough to span a sizable river, and would easily have fitted four London buses side by side. It challenged the imagination to ponder how the snow bridge might hold our weights, but we had no choice but to try.

We prepared a basic belay, and James went first, uncomplaining and apparently nerveless. He even stopped to have a good look on the other side. One by one we followed. When my turn came, I just blotted out all thoughts from my mind, as I shuffled across. This was the worst moment on the worst glacier I had ever crossed.

This was not the end of our troubles. A little further down we had to abseil down a rock step, and the path to the Mer de Glace seemed to have been wiped away by a landslide. Nothing came easy and we were forced to fight every step of the way across the rubble.

On arriving at the Mer de Glace, the route was still far from clear. We had spent the whole afternoon descending the Envers de Plan Glacier and now time was starting to become a factor. The four of us roped up again and set off down the Mer de Glace, wending our way through yet more crevasses.

We lost another hour because of route finding problems, and although there was no friction between us, our indecision was to have consequences. For a while though we made faster progress until Jerry found he had lost a crampon whilst wearing it. He was so tired, he actually hadn't noticed. James admitted having seen a crampon on the ice, but had assumed it was part of the general debris which littered the glacier. The two looked at each other for a moment, but there was nothing we could do about it, and nobody really wanted to go back and look.

The Mer de Glace had a legendary reputation in the 19th century when it was depicted in paintings as being like an ocean of ice in the frenzy of a storm. Now it looked a pale shadow of its former self, and it was quite clear global warming was having its effects. The central parts were largely flat and benign, whilst the moraine and debris at the edges gave it an ugly appearance.

We lost the race against darkness. James and I decided to bivi for the night on some rocks by the right side of the glacier, whilst JR and Jerry elected to continue for a while in the dark, although they were also expecting to have to bivi shortly. Our parting was hasty and not thought through. We kept the rope, which they needed, and they took their bivi bags, which we needed. It was a bitterly cold night. My emergency bivi pack consisted of two plastic bin liners, one of which I gave to James, who was already reminding me that he might have brought his new Gore-tex bivi bag that I had told him wouldn't be required.

We put on every stitch of clothing we had, but still shivered all night. The problem was that our undergarments were damp with perspiration, and these now chilled us to the bone.

To add to the drama, someone was screaming for help from somewhere high on the Dru, across the valley and almost opposite us. There was nothing we could do in this still pre-digital mobile phone era, but shortly afterwards the cries of 'au secours' stopped, and silence returned to the glacier. A few hours later, a helicopter appeared along the far side of the glacier. Initially it seemed to be searching in the wrong place, but then moved over to the Dru, and it was clear a message had reached the rescue services. We never found out what had happened.

It was in the area around where we lay that one of geology's great battles was settled, at least temporarily. It was during the early 1840s that the Swiss, Louis Agassiz, and the Scot, James Forbes, had argued over how glaciers were formed, and had questioned each other's priority in certain discoveries. Forbes, determined to settle the argument once and for all, had decided to spend the summer months of 1842 tramping over, marking and measuring the entire Mer de Glace, including - no doubt - the area where we were now shivering. From this he had produced a book 'Travel through the Alps of Savoy' which explained a lot of what we know about glaciers today and stunned the world of geology at the time, with its insights. Geology in those days, it should be noted, contained some of the leading thinkers of the day.

Fortunately for us the weather remained clear and there was no wind. The hours dragged by, and shortly before dawn James, who was suffering even more than me, suggested we set off. Within fifteen minutes it was light enough to spot the ladders, which we knew were our route of the glacier, and up to Montenvers. I was amazed to see how many other people seem to have biviied on the glacier that night, as they suddenly started appearing all over the glacier. The Midi-Plan traverse had taken James and me some 26 hours and there was no sign of the others.

Back at the campsite we made a quick tent check before lying down ourselves. Relieved to see two human shapes snoring in their sleeping bags, we relaxed somewhat and forgot any thoughts of heading back up for a search. But I was too wound up to sleep, as images of the previous day kept flashing past.

Within an hour I was up, drinking tea, and listening to how JR and Jerry had spent an interesting hour on the glacier in the dark, before meeting a party with head torches and knowledge of where the ladders were. They had walked down to Chamonix, along the railway line and, as proof, their boots were covered in grease from the rack. Their reward, though, had been to eat some chip butties, at two in the morning, whilst we lay shivering in our bin liners, having run out of food and water.

The following 48 hours we rested in Chamonix during the day, and drank beer in the Jeckyl at night. It was during this time I grew to appreciate Chamonix even more. We met up with other British climbers at the campsite, and soon there was a small community of like-minded individuals.

Alec and Richard had been doing serious rock routes, collecting 'Ghastly Rubberfoot' points. These were what we called the numbers given to the top 100 climbs in Chamonix, as selected by the great French climber Gaston Rubbafut. I was quite pleased to find that the Midi-Plan rated 21 on the list. Richard and Alec, however, did two routes that week at the 60-70 level.

One evening, we watched a band called Mukka perform at the Jeckyl and were entranced by their Gipsy style of music. The weather was indifferent during this time, but it was clear an improvement was on the way and we would have time for one more route.

After much discussion it was decided that James and JR would go for Mont Blanc, whilst Jerry and I went for the less exhausting Petit Aiguille Verte. As Mont Blanc was a two-day route, and ours would take only one day, Jerry and I spent an extra day in Chamonix.

The Petit Aiguille Verte is a relatively simple climb from the top of another cable car. It involves only snow plodding until the final rocky ridge, and we were expecting it to be nice and straightforward. The reality proved a little different. Hard ice made the approach to the rock ridge tricky, and then a huge traffic jam built up, which endangered us even more, as people climbed over and under each other's ropes. On our descent we had to wait literally hours for people to move out of our way. If I ever did this route again, I would bivi at the start of the climb to get an early start, rather than catching the first cable car up.

Later that day, James and JR returned from having climbed Mont Blanc. They had taken one look at the crowded Gouter Hut and decided to bivi out in the snow on top of the Aiguille du Gouter, exactly what Tony, Terrence and I should have done eight years before.

That final evening was a pleasant blur. We had just enjoyed two weeks of superb Alpine climbing, including snow and rock, glaciers and bivis. The company had been great, and we had made many new friends. It was also clear, though, that we had sailed close to the wind, and I felt uncomfortable at some of the risks we had taken. I kept these thoughts to myself, however, and was outwardly as cheerful as ever.

Before returning to families, girlfriends and work, we had one final act of pilgrimage to perform. At the local cemetery there was a very special gravestone, one that had been well maintained. It was a tomb unlike any other I had ever seen, a huge piece of rock, mountain-shaped and jagged. We photographed ourselves in situ, and silently paid our own respects to an old master of 'the game', Edward Whymper RIP.

'And the cavalry rode to the rescue.'

'*I told you we were a load
of rubbish James.*'

9. Gaining weight & experience

One autumn evening in 1996, Tony called round to our flat to discuss his forthcoming and long awaited Himalayan trip. The fact that he was going at all was in itself a triumph of will power, and he was full of his usual enthusiasm as he talked about his itinerary. His partner Jane, Jerry - fresh from our summer Alpine trip - and an old school friend of Jane's called Andrew, would accompany him. The four of them would fly to Kathmandu, and set out for Mera Peak (6430m). Almost as an afterthought, Tony asked me if I had some decent windproof gloves he could borrow. I did have a pair, but neither of us was able to find these, despite a good search of my cupboard. After a while Tony told me not to worry, he already had two pairs of Dachstein gloves which he could double up.

Shortly afterwards they were off, and for a few weeks disappeared from my mind. Then I received a phone call from Paul to say there was news.

'I've just heard from Tony.'

'How did it go?' I enquired.

'Not good, he's in hospital again. I'm afraid he's suffering from frostbite to his fingers.'

'Shit, what happened?' I asked.

'I'm not sure. Tony and Jerry made it up Mera peak, but after they returned he and Jane were airlifted out.

Apparently it's serious.'

I couldn't believe it. Not Tony, not again after all he had been through. And suddenly our last meeting took on a new meaning.

A week later Tony was back in London. His fingers were indeed badly frostbitten, something, that had happened, he said, within ten minutes of the start of his summit climb. He had been using trekking poles, and was wearing his two pairs of Dachstein gloves. The cold wind had gone straight through and unbeknown to Tony, his previous injuries to his wrist and arms had restricted the blood flow to his hands and fingers.

'What treatment are you having?' I asked.

'None.' he said, 'I've just got to wait to see how much they recover. It could take some months.'

'Is there nothing else they can do?' I asked.

'No, I've just got to keep things dry.'

Tony remained positive throughout this latest ordeal. He sought advice from Dr Charles Clarke, and also met up with Ed Webster, an American climber who had suffered frostbite injuries during his 1988 Everest climb with Stephen Venables. This seemed to help, and of course his friends also rallied round.

For five months, Tony had wads of cotton wool on the end of his fingers. There were even several funny moments, for example, when we were in a disco in Keswick during Terrence's stag weekend, and saw these cotton wads fluorescing in the dark as Tony danced. On another occasion in France, Tony turned up for a canoeing trip with condoms wrapped around his finger ends!

In the end, he lost the ends of a number of fingers, but fortunately he had naturally long fingers, and they still remained as long as mine at the end of the process. But the operations needed were a nasty reminder of what he had already been through, and this time he promised Jane and himself that he would stop climbing.

Later that spring, Terence and Joanne got married near Southampton. It was a lovely wedding and we celebrated at a great barn dance reception. A short time thereafter Joanne announced she was pregnant. In May we all went to Normandy for the bank holiday. Tony Blair had just won a landslide election, and the country was ready for a new era. Most of us were delighted, and for the first time in our adult lives there was a government, that was not Conservative.

We prepared for our 1997 Alpine campaign as best we could. This involved trips to the Lake District, a weekly visit to the Mile End climbing wall, and a few trips to Wintour's Leap. Again, I found that getting fit was not as easy as it had been in the past. In fact I had never been heavier, and although I went through the motions, I knew deep down that I wasn't really fit enough for the Alps.

This did not mean that I was not keen to return, but more money and a softer lifestyle were having their effects. Agata was working at Harrods and we had never been so well-off.

The usual four, James, JR, Jerry and I, agreed on a two-week trip in late July. Our memories of Chamonix in 1996 led all of us to favour a return. We took two cars, in order to give ourselves maximum flexibility, and met up in the Molliasses campsite late one Friday evening. The following morning we decided we were in the wrong place.

"What's the weather forecast?"

'Seems good for the next day or two.'

'How about the Gran Paradiso? We could drive through the Mont Blanc tunnel and be up at the Vittorio Emanuelle hut tonight?'

'OK but let's leave the tents here. If everything goes to plan, we should be back by tomorrow evening.'

We moved fast and that afternoon, just after midday, we set off from Pont car park for the Vittorio Emanuelle II hut. It was blisteringly hot, and we somehow managed to lose the path, and ended up crossing the river at a difficult place. A little map studying was required to get us back on track, and after that it was only a few more hours before the Vittorio Emanuelle II Hut appeared. This is a most remarkable looking place, as it resembles half a gigantic barrel of beer, whilst inside upstairs in the sleeping quarters, it is like being in the bottom of an old sailing boat.

We relaxed that evening and mentally prepared for the inevitable Alpine start. It nagged at my mind that I had found the short hut climb quite tiring.

Gran Paradiso (4061m) is the highest mountain in the Graian Alps, which lie between the Mont Blanc and the Dauphine. Goedeke described it as *'being far from effortless'* with an *'especially impressive view.'* Two Englishmen and their guides had made its first known ascent in 1860.

We started out at about 4.30am, and made our way in the

dark through a major boulder field. This was the only tricky part, as once it was light, a long snow plod was revealed which snaked up endlessly. I found myself struggling with my rhythm, and started paying the price for my lack of fitness and all the extra weight I was carrying. We slowed down considerably towards the top as I got cramp on a mountain for the first time in my life. The others were very good about it and, in any case, I managed to stagger on.

We reached the summit area inside five hours, which meant, in fact, that we had climbed within guidebook time, but I felt drained. I say summit area because the literal summit was festooned with climbers, rather like those seabirds one sees on nature programmes, covering a South Atlantic island. I think JR actually wriggled his way up the rocky summit steps to touch the statue of the Madonna, but the rest of us could not be bothered. We sat on some rocks overlooking the near vertical looking East Face, a few metres below the Madonna. The view on this fine day lived up to expectations, and it was surprising to see how close Mont Blanc looked to us.

I had not had to fight this hard for a mountain since my flu-ridden ascent of the Lagginhorn four years before, but on looking around saw that I was not in the worst state. Jerry was suffering from exposure, as he had failed to put enough warm clothes on earlier in the day. He couldn't feel his fingers, a threat we were now acutely aware of, and took very seriously. We helped him get some more gear on, and once past the worst he decided to descend immediately.

Jerry shot off down the slopes, and I felt unable to keep up with him. In fact, if he hadn't stopped at a large ledge for a rest, I probably wouldn't have seen him again until I got back to Pont car park. By now he had recovered from his scare, and we all lay on the rocks in the sun, content to be back in the Alps. We had just climbed 2000m to the summit, without any conventional acclimatisation and had worked well together.

The rest of the day represented a steady and relaxed return to our tents in Chamonix. That evening saw us back in the Jeckyl Bar drinking beer. It seemed like the summer of 1996 all over again. Mukka were again due to play and we all collapsed in laughter at Jerry's attempts to chat up the young Irish bar maid. It was a lively evening. We were equally amused when James got a marriage and tent visit proposal, from a woman who looked even older than him!

Waking the following morning with monster hangovers, we staggered down to the guide's office in Chamonix to check the weather forecast. It was not good; a major storm was coming in, and was due to hit the next morning. Slightly crestfallen we retired to a nearby bar to consider our options.

'When's the storm getting here?'

'It said by about mid-morning.'

'Look, what if we go up to the Cosmique Hut this afternoon. If we set off at 4.00am we could be on the summit of Mont Blanc du Tacul by 7.00am and back down to the Midi by 10am, just before the storm.'

We all looked at each other, and I immediately knew the idea had been endorsed. In fact it was our only chance to climb a new 4000m peak in the time available.

'Well if we're going to go up to the hut this afternoon we had better get our arses in gear.'

We raced back to the Molliasses camp site and started packing our gear, which had been left out to dry in the morning sun, and an hour later we were on our way to the Midi cable car.

We had a late lunch, overlooking the cable car, and it was hard to believe the blue skies above were about to give way to a vicious storm. But I had - by now - enough respect for these Alpine weather forecasts not to expect otherwise.

We worked our way down the same exposed snow ridge from the Aiguille du Midi, as we had for our epic day on the Midi-Plan traverse a year earlier. From here it was an easy trudge across to the Cosmique Hut, which we reached by teatime.

It was interesting to note that a party including the reverend Hudson of Matterhorn fame had first climbed Mont Blanc du Tacul (4248m) in 1855. The mountain is not directly attached to its more famous namesake and is an independent 4000m peak in its own right. There were potential dangers. The slopes we would have to climb were known to be avalanche prone, and unstable seracs were a constant threat to parties moving underneath.

The Cosmique Hut was large and spacious, and for the first time ever I paid for my stay and board in an Alpine hut by credit card. After dinner we stood on the terrace at the back of the hut, looking down some major cliffs, and wondered why the hut had been built so close to the edge. In fact, a few years later the hut would indeed fall down over these cliffs.

We never really slept that night, and were up by 3.00am. The hut breakfast in these circumstances is always a quiet affair. People, particularly women, who the night before have seemed rather attractive, suddenly turn up looking twenty years older, something I always found rather amusing.

If some way of measuring enjoyment could be installed at this point in the day, I suspect it would hardly register. Everybody around has bloodshot eyes, bad hairstyles and are all hunched together in uncommunicative groups, displaying a serious pre-occupation with their bowls of muesli. You are tired, sleepy, feeling rough, and about to set out into a dark, cold and dangerous world. Nor would you get any sympathy from the world at large, as this is a self-inflicted torment, which you are, willingly, undertaking during your precious holidays.

But, were some way of measuring the available will power and determination to be found, it would no doubt register near the top of the scale, for almost nobody in the hut ever thinks of quitting. They and you know from experience that it will all be more than worth it – well, probably.

The weather was still holding as we set off at 4.00am, and very shortly after we were following a zig zag route through the seracs. It was noticeably warmer than we were used to at this altitude, and as a consequence the snow was softer. Slowly it became paler and lighter until we could see the incoming weather over to the west. It was clear something unpleasant was on the way and before long the clouds reached us, cutting our visibility to a few yards. We raced onwards, eager not to have our summit denied us at the last moment.

It is natural to think that once you have reached the summit ridge of the Tacul that you are almost home, but this is a deception, particularly when you can barely see the person ahead of you on the rope. It took us a good half hour to climb up the final ridge, and we then faced an interesting 40m climb up a steep snow slope to the summit itself. Again we had done the climb within guidebook time, although this time it was barely more than half the distance we had climbed on the Gran Paradiso.

As we reached the top however, the wind started blowing harder, and it started snowing. Whilst wrapping our rope around the summit cross, I was conscious that it had been frequently battered by lightning strikes, and although outwardly we were all cheerful and full of banter, we all sensed the danger we were in.

It is a fact, however, that if you ever find yourself in a white out on the top of an Alpine 4000m peak, with a major storm approaching, you can derive a good deal of confidence from not only having good quality gear, but knowing you are with three good mates you can rely on. I for example, lost a glove to the wind on the summit, but the others were able to provide a spare.

Our decent was thoroughly unpleasant, as the weather worsened and the snow became powder-like, and balled up under our crampons. Then, through a break in the cloud we saw a long line of people heading towards us far below. They had come up on the first cable car of the day.

'Christ, don't they know there's a storm coming in?'

'Looks like lots of guided parties.'

'They'll never make it. They'll get half way, then turn round and say to their clients: "Shame but there's as storm coming in, we'll have to go down." And they will get paid.'

'I don't blame them really.'

Once down on the lower slopes we passed a few of these parties, still struggling in the soft snow, although most were already turning back. The storm, which was now undoubtedly raging across the summit region, had also started to affect the valley floor and thunder crashed around. We decided not stop at the Cosmique Hut on the way back. We wanted to reach the Aiguille du Midi as quickly as possible, as we were worried that the cable cars might stop running at any moment.

We were moving up the final ridge to the ice cave at the Aiguille du Midi when the storm really got going. I tried not to think of still being out in this weather half way up the route, but knew we had timed our climb almost to perfection. To our relief the cable car was still running and by 10.30am we were drinking large glasses of beer in a Chamonix bar, watching the lighting strikes amidst the pouring rain.

That first day, it was almost fun to watch the rain coming down from the comfort of a warm bar, but then it rained solidly for the next four days. This was discouraging, to put it mildly, and it was made worse by a note I found on the board at the campsite dated the previous week, which described how it had rained every day of the week. It had never even occurred to me it could rain for a week in the Alps in late July, but here was evidence that it could do it for almost two weeks.

'Its all due to global warming you know,' said James.

We had been lucky enough to have arrived in the short spell of good weather in between these two weather fronts and during this time had managed to climb two new 4000m peaks.

Even Chamonix's charms had long faded before we saw the sun again. With plenty of time to study our guidebooks and even read new ones on the shelves of the bookshops in Chamonix, we had a new plan ready for the return of good weather. This involved returning through the Mont Blanc tunnel to Courmayeur and going up to the Torino Hut. From here we would attempt the Tour Ronde (3762m), which caused a certain amount of amusement.

'But Nick it's not a 4000m peak, are you feeling alright?'

'Yeah I know, after four days I don't care about that anymore.'

'But you know this one won't count don't you?'

'Ha ha, very funny.'

The good weather finally arrived and so it happened that we found ourselves a day later heading up a tight and exposed ridge towards the Tour Ronde. Success had been so frequent in recent years that our climbing the ridge seemed almost a foregone conclusion, but it was not to be. We had met a young English guy who was keen to accompany us, and with only one rope between five found we could not get enough pitch space to climb the heavily iced up ridge, with its extremely steep drops.

After some hours of tortuous progress we decided to call it a day. It had been the first summit we had failed to climb as New Team ID, but we were relaxed about it, recognising that another lesson had been learned. The contrast with the previous four days was enough to lift our spirits, and we were given another perspective of this great mountain range. Another thrill once back at the hut was a fine view of the Brenva spur.

On our return to Chamonix we decided it was time for a change of scenery. Zermatt received 'nul points' but James and JR were keen to have a go at the Dom, and this meant a visit to Randa and its very particular campsite. A middle-aged Swiss woman, who was - with hindsight - quite clearly in the midst of some kind of nervous breakdown, was running the place. She exhibited all kinds of very odd and disturbing behaviour. One example of this was when she suddenly screeched and ran over to the table of a fellow Brit from the Alpine Club meet, who were based in the campsite, to berate him for not holding his fork in the 'correct', presumably Swiss, way whilst eating his food. The guy looked stunned, and it was hard not to laugh.

In between all this we camped next to a minivan full of young Polish climbers. They clearly did not have much money, for they slept mostly in the minivan itself, and they had brought their own supply of food with them all the way from Poland. I was impressed by their resilience, and also because about half of them were attractive young women.

That evening we discussed our options. James and JR were still keen to have a go at the Dom. Jerry had decided he didn't fancy it, and I was umming and aaaring. The Dom is the longest climb in the Alps and topped the famous Goedeke 'how much sweat list' with 3160m of ascent. I would have liked to have a go, but deep down I knew I wasn't fit enough. For the first time ever I decided to pass on a major new ascent and it didn't feel good.

The truth was I had eaten too many curries, and had had too many soft days during the winter and spring months. I was now paying the price, and although it was a tough decision to make, I know with hindsight it was the right decision.

Then, just before we turned in for the evening, our Polish neighbours started kitting up, packing their sacks and looking like they were about to set out on a climb. Jerry asked one of the girls what they were planning.

'We're going to climb the Breithorn,' she said.

'Why not wait till morning and take the train,' said Jerry.

'No money,' she replied.

It was impressive, magnificent even. About ten of them set off from Randa campsite, at about 10.00pm intending to climb through the night, and probably most of the next day. First they had to walk to Zermatt, no mean effort, and then work their way up from the valley floor. It made me feel even less impressed with my own fitness, and myself. The more I had learned about the Poles, the more impressed I was. They were a tough, brave and disciplined people, unspoilt as yet in 1997, by the growing softness of Western life.

James and JR left early the next morning aiming to reach the Dom hut before the midday sun got too strong. Jerry and I sat out in the morning sun and discussed our options.

'What do you really want to do?' asked Jerry.

'A couple of easy days out.' I said 'How about we move up to Zermatt now and climb the Breithorn today?'

'Hmmm alright'

'You might even meet up with that Polish girl again.'

'Yes, very funny.'

Within 20 minutes we were packed and ready to go. We drove up to Tasch and then took the train up to Zermatt. A short walk across town and three cable cars later, and we were on the glacier below the Kleine Matterhorn. It had taken less than two hours since we had left Randa.

A further ninety minutes saw us on top of the Breithorn, where we enjoyed the usual fine view of the Zermatt horseshoe. It was my third visit to the top, and we loitered longer than usual before setting off down. Just after reaching the glacier we met up with the Poles.

They were still heading upwards, weary but smiling, and

again for the second time in the past 24 hours I had a feeling of complete inadequacy. Within an hour they would have finished their climb, but I didn't want to think about what time they would finally get back.

That evening in Zermatt, Jerry updated me on his dating adventures, or rather misadventures, for the past six months. It seemed like he had met every single Jewish woman in North London.

'Does it have to be a Jewish woman?' I asked.

'Yes,' he replied.

The following day, we took the train up the Gornergrat intending to have a day out on the Stockhorn. We looked at the Collomb guide, which described the top of the cable car to the summit as being 30 minutes.

'Come on Jerry. Let's try and beat a Collomb guidebook time.' I said.

'I'd be on for that,' replied Jerry.

So we literally started running towards the Stockhorn. We didn't stop, and kept up a completely unnatural pace, that could only be described as a steady jog. Our acclimatisation by now was good, which helped, but even so we were soon suffering. We made the summit, a nice little rock pinnacle, in 28 minutes and collapsed on the rocks.

'So that's what it takes to beat a Collomb guidebook time then.'

'I bet he never came up here,' said Jerry, 'otherwise he would have called it 15 minutes.'

We laughed, and felt we had won back a tiny bit of self-esteem after the Tour Ronde failure, not attempting the Dom and seeing how hard the Poles were.

Late that afternoon, James and JR reappeared in Randa campsite looking very pleased with themselves. They had not only climbed the Dom, but had done it by the slightly harder Festigrat ridge. Both were fit and acclimatised, and had set a fast pace. Apart from the huge effort involved, it had all gone very smoothly, and I was genuinely pleased for them.

We had been sitting for five minutes on the campsite bar terrace listening to tales of their night when they had got off route for a while, and where JR had inadvertently roped himself to a rock face so that he couldn't move, when we were interrupted. The woman running the campsite flew at us, demanding in loud German why we hadn't ordered any drinks yet, and that if we didn't do so immediately we should get off her terrace. This, incidentally, was large and deserted.

We decided to move on to a place down the valley for a drink and meal. The campsite door had a lot of stuck-on messages, forbidding almost everything, including asking to change notes for coins, and too much laughing. As we left next morning, we could not resist adding our own warning to potential campers. The normally fearless James had the car revving, ready for the getaway, whilst one of us stuck a note of complaint on the door.

This was the end of the climbing, and we made our way to stay with some of James' friends - Thierry and Barbi who had a nice house amidst the vineyards overlooking Lake Geneva. On a clear day from their terrace, you could see Mont Blanc in the distance.

They were excellent hosts but, to their amazement, we all opted to bivi out for the night on their terrace despite the fact that it was pouring with rain. It was a real team act.

This bivi, in early August 1997, represented a watershed in our Alpine days in more ways than one. For four summers we had climbed in the Alps together, with one adventure after another. During this time we had reached the summits of nineteen 4000m peaks and a number of 3000m ones too. We had survived dangers, occasionally lived on the edge, and laughed a very great deal. We shared a desire to climb, and had immersed ourselves in the total experience of Alpinism from the greenness below, to the challenges above.

The summer of 1997 saw a record casualty rate amongst Alpinists. Never before had so many fatal accidents occurred in such a short period of time. We were aware of some of this but, remarkably, never openly discussed the 'why' question. Despite my private doubts, however, I knew I felt more alive during these few weeks, than at any other time of the year.

We would continue to climb, but the world around us would

change. New characters would appear, along with older ones, and life would become more complicated. 'The game' would become even more dangerous as global warming began to have its effects. As with the mid 1980s, though, I now look back on this period with a great fondness. The sun didn't always shine, but those memories are burned into my mind forever.

"

'So James, let me get this right.
She told you last night she wanted
to marry you.'

*'That day grown men trembled before the
'Witch of Randa', and fled as fast as
their Mondeo would carry them.'*

10. The family years

The realisation that my current fitness would not allow me to climb the longest Alpine routes, led to the emergence of a new strategy. During those hours on the Stockhorn, I had decided to ask Agata if she would like to climb the Breithorn in the summer of 1998. This much-maligned mountain remains a very fine day out for inexperienced climbers and a great introduction to the Alps. It would also allow me to show her the Alps, about which she had heard a great deal but seen nothing.

After a lot of rock climbing trips during the first few years of our marriage, we had recently taken our family holidays to such places as the Canary Islands and Corfu, whilst also exploring the UK extensively. The one exception had been a two-week camping tour around Europe in 1995 when Agata, Michael and I spent one rainy night in Zermatt, before heading down into Italy.

I discussed the idea with Agata who was interested in having a go. Michael, then aged 13, chose to stay with family in southern Poland for the summer. Our plans developed during the spring of '98.

I still met up with the lads every Thursday night at the Mile End climbing wall, where we discussed the latest news, including that from the climbing world. We had agreed to go on a 'Greater Ranges' trip in 1999, and would therefore skip a year in '98, in order to spend time with our partners.

James, however, expressed an interest in joining forces with us in Zermatt, for a few days with his wife Zoe, who we had known for almost as long as James himself. Their daughter Mia, who was three years younger than Michael, would stay with Thierry and Barbie on the shores of Lake Geneva.

The usual Team ID get-togethers for the Dovedale Dash weekend and the Normandy May bank holiday came and went. It was a time of change and particularly for having babies. Tony and Jane, for example, had bounced back from their Himalayan ordeal by announcing that Jane was pregnant again.

That autumn Rhiannon was born and I was invited to be her godfather. Then Terrence and Joanne, who had married in early 1997, announced that they too would have a baby that Christmas. Eleanor was indeed born a few days before the end of the year. Again I was invited to be a godfather. When Liz then gave birth to Anna, it seemed that 'girl power' ruled.

These additions meant a complete change of atmosphere during our weekends away. There was no more camping or exclusive focus on the pub at nights. More and more we sought out gites or barns where we could all stay together. Nights felt shorter, babies cried and less alcohol was consumed.

This was the time of the Monica Lewinsky affair when Bill Clinton was on the 'Starr rack' in front of the world's media. For a while it even looked like he might have to resign.

Moreover, we were getting wealthier. The economy in Britain was growing fast and for the first time, I had a property that was worth more than I had paid for it.

In the spring of 1998, I went on a three-day business trip to Annecy and the surrounding areas with customers. I was impressed, and afterwards suggested to Agata that we should start our week's holiday here.

It was a successful week. Starting in Annecy, we made our way over to Chamonix. Approaching from this side gave a striking view of Mont Blanc, which Agata was seeing for the first time. We camped in the Molliasses campsite and visited the main sites of Chamonix. We also spent a few hours up at the Aiguille du Midi, where we sat in the sun and watched climbers completing the Cosmique Arête. This route really caught my imagination and I stored it away for future reference.

The following day we made our way to Zermatt, where we met up with James and Zoe in the campsite. We took a picnic by the lakes on the way up to the Hornli Hut, and talked about life and our plans. We had intended to spend the following day up on the Gornergrat acclimatising, but the weather forecast was ambiguous, so we decided to gamble on the Breithorn the next day.

Although the Breithorn is seen as a soft touch, people have

nevertheless died on its slopes. In 1913 a German doctor froze to death when his guide lost his bearings in poor weather and in the 1980s five skiers had undergone a similar fate. We knew we needed to be prepared and careful of bad weather.

In the event it took us two hours to get from the summit of the Kleine Matterhorn to the top of the Breithorn. Unfortunately cloud obscured our views but it was a great moment to be sitting on the top of a 4000m peak with our wives. Both Zoe and Agata were delighted and we were even serenaded by a trumpeter who played for a few minutes in the thin air. But I was dismayed to find my own fitness had declined significantly since the year before, and the whole outing was far more tiring than it should have been, even allowing for a lack of acclimatisation.

On the way down Zoe too began to suffer from altitude sickness. The last part of this Breithorn descent always seems further than you expect, particularly on softening snow.

We stopped off for a drink and early lunch at the Trockener Steg, which has a superb view of the North Face of the Breithorn. Zoe soon recovered here, and we were all smiling in the hot sun. The magic of the Alps held us all that afternoon, proof it was not just for a few hardened climbers.

On returning home, I made a decision. I would lose my surplus weight and get back to my fitness of ten years before. The alternative meant giving up climbing, because after struggling to climb the Breithorn, I was unlikely to climb anything much harder and longer again.

I started my diet immediately, and began visiting the gym three times a week. Slowly things improved and within six months I had lost a large amount of weight and was ready to start jogging again. By the summer of 1999 I was running half marathons every weekend and was back to 1980s weight levels. I felt better than I had done for many years, with more energy, mentally sharper and completely re-enthused.

We were still meeting at the Mile End climbing wall every Thursday evening, and then going to a local curry house afterwards. One day Richard announced he had met a French lawyer called Ana-Maria. They were soon engaged and the wedding was set for the autumn of 1999, to be held in Greece.

This was also the time of the Kosovo air campaign, which continued for 78 days. My other key memory of this period was the power of the Internet, which, by now, had developed from its early days into an amazing tool. Real time information was now available beyond TV and radio.

1999 was to be the year of our greater ranges trip. We had planned for three weeks, and initially considered the Himalayas. However, Nepal required an April/May or October/November timing and this was simply not practical with our jobs. To take three weeks required an August destination, which was the standard British holiday month. We considered the Mountains of the Moon in Uganda, and Mt Elbrus in the Caucasus, and even the Canadian Rockies, but they were rejected as being too wet, too politically unstable, or not high enough, in that order. Realistically this left the Andes, and it was now that we remembered Jerry's time in Bolivia in 1993.

We asked Jerry for more details and he confirmed not only his enthusiasm for Bolivia but also his willingness to return. We contacted a climber called Yossi Brain, in La Paz, and he organised some local support for us. In the end seven of us set off for South America in early August 1999. The team consisted of James, JR, Jerry, Rory, Andrew and his wife Carol, and me.

On the flight over James collapsed and needed oxygen. Our concern however changed to amusement, when the attractive American stewardess, Anna, who had been looking after him, gave him her personal address details. James' recovery was swift.

It was a fascinating trip and very successful in terms of summits. We camped at Condoriri and climbed Mirador (5226m), following this up with a direct climb up the glacier of Tiraja (5060m). After a rest day, we climbed Huayna Potosi (6088m), taking two days, including a bivi above 5000m. Here we narrowly missed being caught up in an avalanche which swept our route shortly after we had crossed, killing two climbers. We scrambled up the last part of Chacaltaya (5392m), which has a road up most of it and then travelled to the Chilean border where Andrew and JR climbed Sajama (6520m). James reached 6200m before turning back and I was prevented from attempting it because of a nasty dose of giardia.

During our final week we went to Peru and visited Macchu Picchu. There was a train strike at the time, so we flew in by helicopter, courtesy of the Peruvian army. One amusing memory was Andrew outraging some Americans, by stating that his junior school was older than Macchu Picchu, in a tone suggesting disinterest.

I returned to Britain, still not fully recovered from my stomach bug and weighing less than I could ever remember. Bolivia had been a tremendous experience, with great people and a fascinating capital, although we had liked Peru far less. Global warming had also been clearly evident with the glacier and snowfields of Chacaltaya, once the highest skiing area in the world, having disappeared during the past 30 years. But I had to admit that scenically I had been disappointed with those parts of the Andes we had seen. There was very little colour in that harsh brownish environment, and surprisingly little white, for the snow line was very high. Because of the greater altitude of the valley floors, the Andean peaks appear no higher than those in the Alps. I decided that I preferred Africa to South America with its warmth, colour and vibrancy.

We had only been back a month, when the sad news came through that Yossi Brain had been killed by an avalanche. We sent a message of condolence. It was another reminder of how dangerous climbing could be.

As we approached the change of the millennium, I accepted a job offer to move to the Netherlands. This was due to start in the spring of 2000 and it meant that we would have to say goodbye to the UK. Our friends were incredulous, and leaving them was the hardest wrench, but in truth after thirteen years I was tired of living in London. Our new destination, Eindhoven in the south of the Netherlands, was only about five hours by car to London. Had we been moving to Manchester or Newcastle we would have been just as far away.

In a grand farewell tour Agata and I went to the Lake District before New Year's Eve, and climbed Scafell Pike. We visited several favourite places, and I knew the area I would miss most in the UK would be the North West. We were not leaving because of a lack of pride. During the past two decades I had witnessed a major revival in Britain's economic, political and social fortunes. The 1970s seemed like – and were - a distant, bad memory.

I managed to sort out one more thing before leaving. For some years I had wanted to join the Alpine Club. At one stage this had seemed impossibly far away, a place for the big names of British climbing, and not for 'ordinary Joes' like me. But as time went by, and my list of ascents grew, the idea seemed more attainable.

'Why bother joining?' I was asked by more than one of my friends.

I had listed the many attractions. To my mind, they are that here is a club full of like-minded individuals. Also there are the meets, the lectures, the newsletters, an annual copy of the Alpine Journal, discounts in Alpine huts and the bunkhouse in central London, even if you did have to be on club business to stay there. As an historian, I was also fascinated by the idea of access to the extensive library. Nor did it cost very much.

To me, the reasons were convincing but my friends remained indifferent. The Alpine Club had been set up in 1857 for the 'promotion of good fellowship among mountaineers, of mountain climbing and mountain exploration throughout the world, and of a better knowledge of mountains through literature, science and art'. It was the first such club in the world. The timing had been good and its membership had grown rapidly. Within a few decades it was an institution, to which most of the great names of British climbing world at the time, and since, have belonged.

One of my favourite stories was a quote from the 1914 Alpine Journal, which compared without irony the so called 'democratic' nature of the continental Alpine Clubs to that of the British.

'The Swiss Alpine Club now numbers 13,496 members, The German and Austrian 100,023, the Italian 7500, the French

6,500 and the British about 730'

Over the years, and away from the mountains, the Club's clashes, between the great egos of the age became legendary, with blackballing, threatened lawsuits, and temper resignations, all providing fascinating additional chapters to the club's history. Some of the reasons seem banal today. Examples include the mis-spelling of names or the obsessive checking of the facts behind a written report to discover possible inaccuracies. Today, fortunately, things are different with there being a thriving active membership coming from 30 countries.

The main problem was that I was not sure I knew anyone in the club, and the rules of entrance demanded that I not only have a proposer but a seconder. I started attending lectures at the Club's quarters in Charlotte Road in central London, often with Richard, and met the then secretary, Glyn Hughes.

I then remembered Kate Phillips from my student days. Kate, who was a member of the Alpine Club, had occasionally joined us for days out on the crags. I had not seen her since the early 1990s but wrote to her asking if she would be willing to propose me. She did, and Glyn offered to second me, so I joined in early 2000.

Agata, Michael and I emigrated to the Netherlands at the start of April 2000. Despite the fact that the steepest hill in my area was the local underpass, we were in many ways fortunately placed. A few hours away lay the Ardennes, whilst I could be on the Swiss border in five hours. And Eindhoven had a good indoor climbing wall. It felt appropriate to be starting a new life in a new country at the start of a new century.

Whilst I started a new job at Philips, Michael who was by now 15, attended the International School. He had not initially wanted to leave the UK but soon warmed to the idea. Agata busied herself learning Dutch, which she managed in a remarkably short time.

Working in the Netherlands, I now had an incredible 38 days holiday per year, not including bank holidays, and could not imagine being able to take it all. The Netherlands offered us a far higher quality of life than we had had in London, although in some areas, such as retailing and banking, the Dutch were a long way behind the UK.

With all this holiday, Agata and I had both wanted to climb Kilimanjaro that summer, but it soon became clear that neither James and Zoe, nor JR and his new girlfriend Lorenda could take the necessary two to three weeks off. Then Richard suggested a family week in the Alps, and we agreed to throw it open to our friends. In the end, 25 people signed up and we had to hire two chalets in Saas Fee to fit everyone in.

Agata and I decided to visit the Dolomites before joining the others in Switzerland. She had heard many tales of our 1994 visit, and we planned to do some walking and a Via Ferrata or two. We drove down to Cortina in late July without having to worry about a ferry or tunnel crossing. Again the first few days were a reminder of the past. We stayed in the same campsite in Cortina, ate the same excellent pizzas, and walked all over the Cinques Torri.

We decided to have a go at the Ivano Dibona route on Monte Cristallo, which was part of the Cristallo massif, and described by our guidebook as an *'interesting and scenically very impressive route'*. It was graded C which meant some previous experience was required along with surefootedness and freedom from vertigo. I had no qualms that Agata who had climbed VS before would be able to make it, but she needed the right gear. We therefore stopped at a local climbing shop to acquire a full Via Ferrata harness and clips.

A Via Ferrata is a rock route, which has been equipped with metal cables, and stanchions, and sometimes also ladders and rope bridges. The idea is that you wear a harness and clip into the metal cables, thus ensuring your protection whilst you move along the route. You have two clips so that you can always clip the next part before removing the existing clip, and you can therefore remain secured at all times.

The theory sounds foolproof but, in reality, dangers still remain. Wire ropes can become damaged, protection may be missing which means you will be effectively soloing, whilst in poor conditions ice and lighting are threats. It is, of course, common sense not to go on a Via Ferrata in anything but very good weather. But we were very aware that storms can still appear fast, and delays could lead to trouble.

We took the cable car to the Forcella Staunies, a hut at the start of the climb. The cable car was left over from the 1930s and had a distinctly thin and rusty looking bottom, which left us giggling nervously. Local guides had laid out our well-protected route in 1969. It goes along rock walls with cables on good paths, over ridges and gorges, through ravines, over wooden bridges and up iron ladders. The route is now named after a local guide who in 1969 had fallen to his death here with his client.

It turned out to be extremely exposed, with climbing up to III including ladders and a rope bridge. Agata was far from happy, but she soldiered on gamely and after some hours we reached the summit of the Cristallino d'Ampezzo (3008m). Here we attracted a large number of birds, which added to the menace of the sensational drops around us. I took a photo of her but she refused to smile.

'I hate you.' was all Agata would say.

Adding to the interest was the fact that the summit ridge had been the Italian front line in the First World War, and was studded with dugouts and caves. From 1915 – 17 the south side of the Cristallo swarmed with Austrian and Italian Alpine troops, who dug themselves into the rocks and built barracks, cableways for materials, trenches, barbed wire entanglements and gun emplacements. More than 80 years had passed since this Alpine war, but its traces were still clearly visible.

It took some time to get back to the Forcella Staunies Hut at the start of the route and I remember thinking what a wonderful route this was. Once back at the hut Agata demanded a double brandy, whilst I had a cup of tea. It had been a great day out.

In order to compensate for this overdose of adrenalin, I suggested a visit to Venice and we spent a couple of romantic days on the Italian coast. This was a perfect mixture of mountains and culture.

The team ID Saas Fee week was a wonderful gathering. Our pair of chalets were 50m apart. With James, Zoe, their daughter Mia and her friend Jenny, we visited the Hohaas Hut and went to the edge of the Weismiess Glacier. From here we descended to the Weismiess Hut.

The following day, Richard, Ana-Maria and I climbed the chossy North Face of the Mittaghorn (3200m), which stands out clearly above Saas Fee. It was loose, and involved scrambling at about grade II. We didn't carry a rope but once committed none of us felt like going down. At the summit we chose to descend down the other side. A rope would have been useful, and we were lucky to find a way down through the cliffs.

Saas Fee, which like Zermatt is car-free, was made for our group. We lapped up the bars and restaurants and my favourite attraction was the swimming pool with a great view of the Allalinhorn.

This was our next day out, when most of the group headed up to the MittelAllalin. James and Mia, Jerry, Paul, Richard and Ana-Maria, Agata and I set off to climb the Allalinhorn. Mia, then aged 12, got within 150m off the summit before being forced to give up, but the rest of us continued on to the top. It was Agata's second 4000m peak, and this time she got the excellent view we had hoped for.

The following day we all travelled around to Zermatt and up to the Gornergrat, where we sat out in the sun admiring the Matterhorn. Tony was in great form, laughing and joking. Jane had recently given birth to their third child, Matthew, and it was good to see how they had overcome so many obstacles in putting their lives back together. Tony had started cycling. This was an activity in which he could push himself without putting too much pressure on his joints and he had regained most of his former physique. I contrasted his persistent drive, with my own recent sloth.

We walked down to the Riffelalp station cutting across the open green spaces above the tree line. I carried Rhiannon on my shoulders, and we enjoyed an afternoon walk. Here was another side to the Alps, the enjoyment below the snowline, with family and friends. Marketa also made her way down with us on her crutches. Hers was the real triumph of spirit that day, and we were all amused when she finished the descent in a wheelbarrow pushed by Jerry in a successful effort not to miss the last train back.

That afternoon before we headed back to Saas Fee we all had a drink in the North Wall Bar. I had so many memories here, of evenings either before or after climbs, that it felt good to be able to add one involving the families and kids, in this part of 'the game'.

After returning to our chalets we had a famous party. We came in fancy dress, made our own music with pots and pans and danced late into the night. After a few hours I went and sat out on the terrace of our hut overlooking the valley. It was dark and the lights in the valley twinkled below. I was with a great group of friends and life felt good. The Alps are not just about climbing, but can be enjoyed by families too. Shortly though, my Alpinism was about to get a whole lot more complicated.

'In which Jerry helped Marketa catch
the last train home.'

1995 – Monch team, L-R: Brother Will, Jerry, the author, James. Taken on our acclimatisation day.

1996 – New Team ID on the summit of the Signalkuppe L-R, Jerry, the author, JR, James. Taken just after our ice slope epic.

1996 – James biviing in a bin-liner on the Mer de Glace – he is pretending to sleep.

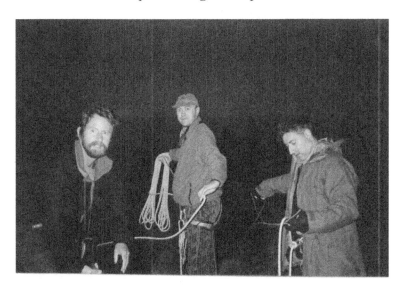

1996 – A classic Alpine start on Monte Rosa. L-R James, JR, Jerry.

1997 – James during our failure on the Tour Ronde.

1998 – Zoe left and Agata right on the summit of the Breithorn - a fine day out.

2000 – Summit Allalinhorn with L-R Ana-Maria, JR, Lorenda, Paul, Jerry, Agata, the Author.

2001 – Late afternoon, well below the Tracuit hut we hit soft snow - taken during our weekend ascent of the Bishorn.

2005 – Crossing the Bergshrund Barre des Ecrins.

2002 – Agata & Katie on the Grand Balcon Sud – Chamonix.

2005 – The author and Hugo finish the Cosmique Arête, Aiguille du Midi Chamonix.

2005 – Summit Dome de Neige des Ecrins, just before the storm, L-R JR, Nick, Hugo and James.

2007 – The Mer de Glace was melting fast.

11. Weekend Alpinism

Towards the end of 2000, Agata became pregnant with our second child. This was a hugely exciting event, which fully occupied our minds for the next nine months. It would also have significant consequences for my trips to the Alps and my attitude to them.

Balancing fatherhood again with Alpinism was a dilemma. I knew it would be a long time before I would be able to go back to the Alps for a few weeks climbing. However, there was one way in which I could still have my 'Alpine Strudel', as it were, and eat it.

The 'Alpine summit in a weekend' was not a new idea, even for Team ID. Back in 1991, Terrence and Tony, funded by the European Newspaper and hence, as we now know, the Maxwell pension funds, had 'done' the Eiger in just this way. Moreover, in subsequent years, I had heard of other parties climbing the Matterhorn in a similar manner.

Now, ten years later, I sought to revive the idea as it seemed my only option that summer and probably for several summers to come. It meant little or no acclimatisation, but allowed for a concentrated burst of energy and enthusiasm.

The idea hit fertile ground, as James and JR were planning a major family trip to Kilimanjaro in August 2001, and did not have time for a week in the Alps either. Jerry too had plans, and the three of them agreed to a long weekend in mid June. This, in itself, was a gamble, as we had never been this early in the season before, and it was quite possible we would spend the entire weekend ensconced in the bars.

Under these circumstances, it might have been prudent to select an easy short climb, but instead - in our bravado - we selected the Bishorn (4153m). Its 2450m of ascent made it the eighth longest route in the Alps, and the absence of cable cars meant it had to be climbed from the valley floor. It would also mean a new valley and a new mountain.

The Bishorn is a two-day climb from Zinal, with the Tracuit

Hut (3256m), which might or might not be open, situated at the top of the Turtmann Glacier. It had officially been climbed for the first time by a British and Swiss team in 1884.

Five players signed up for this new challenge, JR, Jerry, James, Richard and I. Richard had by now completed his retraining, and was a fully practising barrister. As a result of this, we were to be accompanied by a sixth unseen person, namely Richard's Judge, as they both absolutely had to be in court in London on Monday morning.

We would be meeting at Geneva airport on Friday morning and Richard's return flight was Sunday evening. JR and I would drive from the Netherlands on Thursday evening and arrive in Geneva so as to meet the others early the next morning.

Everything went smoothly, and despite the car being as full as I remember any car with five guys and their gear, we arrived at Zinal (1680m) at about 2.00pm that afternoon. To our delight, the weather forecast was miraculously good for the next three days. Getting our priorities right, we immediately set off for a local restaurant for a major slap up meal. I must confess to having some doubts at this stage but the others were full of drive and enthusiasm and it was decided to start on the 1580m hut climb at 16.30pm. Comments by the waitress that the route up to the hut was impassable with soft snow and that the hut was probably not yet open were ignored.

Richard was a driven man on a tight schedule, and we joked that he was living in fear of the 'Judge'. So heavily laden, and complete with sleeping bags, food, gas and stoves, we set off and made steady progress upward for three hours. Then we reached the snowline, and we found ourselves sinking in up to our knees. Further progress was incredibly hard work.

Another three hours later, it was getting dark. We were nowhere near the hut and our progress would have been categorized as slow even on the upper slopes of Everest. At 11.30pm I decided to bivi for the night on a rocky slope, and James volunteered to share this experience with me. This time at least we had Gore-tex bivi bags with us. The 'Judge', however, jabbed Richard in the kidneys, and JR and Jerry, neither of whom fancied biviing, kept on going, and reached the Tracuit Hut after a further three hours.

Although James and I were warm, it was an uncomfortable night because of the slope we were on and I spent most of it planning to descend in the morning. These thoughts however were immediately dispelled when I stuck my head out of my bivi bag, and saw a clear blue-skied morning. James and I made our way up to the Tracuit Hut in 45mins, to find the others asleep, the only occupants of the hut.

Suddenly and improbably the summit was on again. That Saturday we rested all day. Richard was still restless. It was as if the 'Judge' was slapping him on the forehead every few minutes, but he still reckoned he had time to summit and get back to Geneva airport in time for his 7pm flight Sunday evening. He set his non-negotiable turn around time as 8.30am.

At 2.50am that Sunday morning we stepped out of the hut, for the 900m climb to the summit. Had we maintained the Goedeke guidebook time we might have reached the summit before first light, but the conditions above were even worse than below the hut. After 10 metres we were sinking past our knees into the snow and occasionally it was thigh deep. Higher up, it was a little better but each step needed to be kicked for there was no existing trail.

At first light we were still working our way up the otherwise easy slopes. The weather remained good but the effort was draining, and at this stage Jerry decided he would prefer his 'bivi en route ploy' and we left our ropes with him. He was soon sitting confidently in his Gore-tex bag, clearly hoping for the miraculous appearance of some young eligible women.

Richard was a man possessed, and kicked all the steps for the next 500m and two hours. We gratefully followed and I was quite sure that, without this ready-made trail I would have been forced to join Jerry.

Towards the summit, however, even Richard's phenomenal energy levels began to run out, and he started to slow down. At 8.30am, after a total of 40 hours ascent from Zinal, and only about ten minutes from the summit, Richard turned round and announced he had run out of time and needed to go down. The

'Judge' had clearly 'gone for the balls'.

At 8.50am, I followed James to the summit to find JR waiting. He said he would race down after Richard and see if he needed a lift from the valley to the railway station some 20km away. This he did but only caught up with him at the hut, and with the 'Judge' as cheerleader, the two of them raced down to the valley.

Here they discovered that the bus Richard was banking on was not running, and JR offered to drive Richard for 45minutes to the local station. JR then drove back up the valley and, after knocking back a beer, was surprised to feel a little knackered. It was mid-afternoon and he was expecting to see us appear any moment.

Whilst this was taking place, James and I remained on the summit taking it easy. Our own timetable merely required us to be near Geneva that evening, and we relished the view of the Grand Gendarme on the ridge between the Bishorn and the Weisshorn. A few hours earlier I would have gladly settled for an ascent of the Bishorn's East summit otherwise known as Point Burnaby (4135m), but now I barely glanced at it as we descended.

We lost height rapidly, met up with Jerry and the three of us slowly re-crossed the Turtmann Glacier. We arrived back at the hut just before 11.00am. Here we opted for an hour's sleep before descending further and I remember setting the alarm for 12.00 then going straight to sleep. Waking up seemed only a moment later when the alarm went off.

It seemed to help, which was just as well as our descent to Zinal took another six hours. Our leisurely pace was enforced by fatigue but it also gave me time to take in the valley, which was more barren and deserted than its neighbour, the Matterdal. It was probably the absence of cable cars that kept it this way, a small reminder of the Alps as previous generations would have known them.

We finally met up with JR just before 6pm. He was less than amused to hear we had slept at the hut. Even after his heroics though, he was still strong enough for the two-hour drive to the other side of Lake Geneva. I just sat in the back feeling numb, and munching a large bag of crisps.

It took some time for the past few days to sink in. That night we again dined at Thierry and Barbie's lovely home among the vineyards overlooking Lake Geneva, and watched the sun go down – all accompanied with several glasses of fine wine from the attached vineyard. It seemed a fitting finale for a tremendous weekend, in which we had taken on long odds and somehow won through.

That night, despite the fact I had barely slept since leaving the Netherlands, I found sleep hard to come by. We had been through such a roller coaster of emotions during the previous days. I was acutely aware that it was only Richard's energy, which had made it happen. It was an injustice that he had not made the summit himself, but at least he was on time for his appointment in court on the Monday morning. It's amazing how much can be achieved in a weekend, if you don't waste any of it on sleep.

In August 2001 Agata gave birth to our beautiful healthy daughter Katie. It was an emotional moment, but this soon gave way to exhaustion, as Katie turned out to be both a poor sleeper and a demanding baby. She was also a lovely baby, but we needed help from Agata's mother Helena, and also my own mother, in order to get by.

A month later 9/11 happened. In an experience typical of many, I watched the rolling news on a large TV in our coffee corner at work. A large crowd of international colleagues gathered, and there was a sense of shock and disbelief. After the first tower collapsed I returned to my desk to try to work in order to take my mind off the events.

2002 turned into a very hard year, mainly due to Katie's sleeping habits. She rarely slept for more than a few hours at a time, and both Agata and I were soon exhausted. I took to finding empty meeting rooms at work in which to have short catnaps, whilst Agata did shifts at home with the two grandmothers.

Despite this, or maybe because of this, I managed two

Alpine trips that year. In early July we had another Team ID long weekend in the Alps. This time we travelled to Zermatt, our target a climb of Pollux. I drove down with a Dutch friend Ronald Dalderup, with whom I had climbed Sugar Loaf Mountain in Rio the year before during a business trip.

We met James and his brother Hugo, JR and Jerry in Zermatt campsite. It was our first visit to Zermatt together as a climbing team since the rain of 1994, and Hugo's first Team ID trip.

We were again blessed with superb weather as we set out for the Kleine Matterhorn. We had decided as a novelty to hire some snowshoes - Canadian style - for the glacier, and were heavily laden with bivi gear and supplies. My fitness was by now as poor as it had ever been and I was overweight and tired. All this should have been a warning.

Once on the glacier we decided to nip up the Breithorn before heading down the glacier and biviing as close to the Zwillingsjoch as possible. Jerry, who was already feeling the altitude, and was sick, decided to remain on the glacier whilst the rest of us plodded up the familiar and easy-angled Breithorn slopes.

Soon I was gasping for breath and feeling wretched. I managed to drop my rucksack, which JR retrieved for me and only reached the top with great difficulty, just as the others were getting worried about me. Our emotions were variously a mixture of delight, impatience and disinterest. Ronald was delighted with his first 4000m summit, whilst James, JR and Hugo were keen to move down the glacier towards Pollux, and I just wanted to get down to Zermatt.

Back on the glacier, we decided that Jerry and I would go back down, whilst the others would head on and get as far as possible before biviing. The sun beat down on us mercilessly, and it was a real struggle to get back to the cable car on the softening snow. It was all a far cry from a year before. I had forgotten to respect the Alps and was in no shape to climb 4000m peaks. Complacency had been punished.

That night, Jerry and I found ourselves eating out in Zermatt again, whilst the others were on a route.

'Well Jerry, tell me about some of your latest dates?'

But the others were back too by late morning. They had staggered on before finally biviing for the night on the glacier. After a comfortable night they had woken feeling superstitious, and had decided not to have a go at Pollux. Like us they had that 'panda eyed' look from extremely sunburnt faces. The weekend had been pleasant but held none of the drama of the previous year. The highlight was the lads' bivi, which had been wild, remote and beautiful, and worthwhile in its own right.

The second trip to the Alps was a Team ID family week in Chamonix, about a month later. Some thirty of us including kids rented a rather nice house near central Chamonix for a week. It was also Katie's first trip to the Alps, although she would not remember any of it. In fact, she would celebrate her first birthday while we were there.

The weather was unkind but we still managed to do a lot. We all traversed the Grand Balcon Sud, a kind of low-level Midi Plan traverse, which ended at Montenvers, which Katie completed, in a rucksack. We managed some rock climbing one day, and James and JR disappeared early one morning to climb the Petit Aiguille Verte. Agata had also wanted to go parascending and Katie and I watched her run off a cliff with an instructor opposite Mont Blanc early one fine morning. By some quick work and with help from the chair lift and car, we were able to meet her as she landed in Chamonix.

Each evening, a different couple would do the cooking, and we had girls' and boys' nights out when our partners would do the babysitting. We talked and laughed a lot and although our faces were by now becoming middle-aged I sensed the same vitality we had had twenty years before. The holiday reconfirmed our view that the Alps are a tremendous destination for family holidays in summer. This was in addition to winter skiing trips.

Katie remained a demanding child throughout the next year. We tried to compensate for the stress, by going on luxury holidays, skiing in Canada and having a week in Mexico but this only brought a temporary respite.

Despite this, life in the Netherlands was good. We had a nice four-bedroom house, something we could never have afforded in London and it was great to be able to be in Belgium in half an hour and Germany in sixty minutes. Weekends in the Ardennes, the Rhine valley, Flemish Cities or even Paris were possible.

I took a number of work colleagues rock climbing in Belgium, where the bolted routes made for an enjoyable experience. Here I watched young people climbing routes alongside me using rope and belay techniques that I did not recognise, but which relied on there being solid belays in situ. It was impressive to see but I wondered how they would cope on climbs without bolts, such as those in the UK or the Alps.

That March the second Gulf War started and, although the war itself was surprisingly short, the aftermath would go on for years. The 'end of history' quote from a decade before was beginning to seem laughable.

At home the Dutch people were friendly and open and there was a thriving international community. Virtually everyone spoke English and the prices of most things were lower than London, although the introduction of the Euro definitely made things more expensive. We still visited England at least three times a year to meet up with friends for a much needed curry. I discovered to my amazement that although curry is an acquired taste, you also lose the ability to eat hot curries very quickly when you don't get a chance to practise.

Then in the early summer of 2003 I got a call from Richard.
'Have you seen there's a new version of Goedeke out?'
'No.'
'Well he's added a lot of new summits, it's based on the new UIAA list.'
'So how many are there now?'
'Eighty-two I think, and Goedeke thinks there should be nine more on top of that.'
'Whaaattt?'

This was an interesting development. For years we had ignored the arguments raging around the way Alpine summits were classified and had stuck with a list of sixty-one which represented *'the traditional German speaking perspective'*. Now with the addition of twenty-one new summits our percentage of 4000m peaks climbed had dropped from more than a third to barely a quarter. Not only this, but one of the original Goedeke summits listed, the Balmenhorn, had been demoted to the second division, and wouldn't count anymore whilst those peaks which had been added, with few exceptions, seemed to be jagged, sharp and hard.

In a sense this was academic because I had long accepted we would not be able to complete all the Alpine 4000m summits. A significant number were simply too hard for us, at least without guides, and this I refused to contemplate. We still stubbornly held on to the idea that we wanted to achieve our climbs by ourselves, without outside help. And if that meant we wouldn't climb the Aiguille Blanche then so be it. There was irony though in the thought that not only were the mountains themselves moving, through plate tectonics and erosion, but so were the man-made definitions of what those mountains were.

The lads were planning a three-week trip to Ladakh to climb Stok Kangri (6121m). I declined the trip for cost and time reasons but also because I felt uncomfortable visiting the region after the Iraq war. In the end James, Jerry, Rory, Hugo and a German friend called Ivo went and climbed the mountain. I remember hearing about one amusing incident at least. During the summit push, Jerry had tired and decided to bivi en route again, and await the return of the others. He lay down in the dark in his bivi bag, all zipped up, and after a while spotted a solo climber climbing up. As the guy came level to where he was lying, Jerry suddenly sat up and said 'good morning'. The solo climber almost fell off, with shock!

As an alternative, I walked the Hadrian's Wall trail from Wallsend to the other side of Carlisle with JR, Lorenda and Terrence. It was a great week and I met JR's parents in

Newcastle. They were very fine people with a host of stories and an immense cheerfulness, courage and fortitude.

I flew back to the Netherlands and decided to drive via Zermatt on my way to meet up with Agata and Katie in Poland. Zermatt was suffering from a heat wave and the temperature had just reached 37°C. I had planned to camp but on a sudden impulse decided to see if there were any cheap last minute hotel deals. I had been to Zermatt eight times before but had never stayed anywhere other than the campsite. To my surprise I was offered a four star hotel near the North Wall Bar for the equivalent of £40 a night plus breakfast. I took it.

The following day I climbed the Breithorn by myself. As expected, in the circumstances, it was extremely icy and the bergshrund was harder than I had ever experienced. The summit slopes were all ice, and for the first time I became really aware of the effects of climate change in the Alps. Not only was it hotter than ever before, but there had also been a major rockslide on the Matterhorn, and the Hornli Ridge was shut to climbers.

However there was one pleasure still waiting. On returning late that morning I walked into my hotel, went to my bedroom and ran a bath. I then soaked for an hour in the hot water and made a mental note to finish a climb this way more often. It was interesting to experience, albeit in some small way, the lifestyle of the Victorian pioneers.

There were also significant family developments later that summer. Michael had passed his IB exams with a good score of 31 and, despite having a university place at London University, was keen to study in Florida with his girlfriend. We supported his decision and saw him off at Brussels airport.

Later that autumn came the great news that Terrence and Joanne were going to have another child. Poppy was born in December, and would prove to be as lively as Katie had been. John and Liz now had three kids, Anna, Tom and Katie and young children now dominated our get-togethers.

One Saturday morning that November, I watched England win the Rugby World Cup. As Jonny Wilkinson slotted over his winning kick, my shouts of joy were so loud I woke Katie and got an instant telling off from Agata. But spending the next few hours babysitting was a very small price to pay.

By 2004 our domestic situation had improved to the extent that we could at least expect full nights sleep. Early in the year we had decided to go to Kilimanjaro around Christmas with some Polish friends to celebrate Agata's 40th birthday. This left me with little room for a major Alps trip that summer, so again I turned to the 'convenience' of weekend Alpinism.

James, his brother Hugo, and some of their mates were determined to have a go at the Matterhorn and had planned a week in early July. I decided to organise a long weekend at the start of their visit and set about recruiting people. Neither JR nor Jerry could make it but my brother Will expressed an interest and Ronald, plus Marek Stawinski, a Polish friend all signed up. The four of us drove down early one Friday morning and were established in Zermatt campsite later that afternoon. The weather forecast was good with blue skies and sunshine. Shortly after James and Hugo arrived with their mates, Dermot and Paul, and the North Wall Bar did good business that night.

The following morning, we left for the Breithorn. My fitness was a little better than it had been a few years before but, in reality - with three inexperienced friends - the Breithorn was the only realistic 4000m peak within our grasp. James and Hugo's party had initially been sceptical but decided to join us 'for acclimatisation.'

We raced up the by now familiar slopes, and reached the summit en masse. It was Marek's first 4000m summit, and he was delighted. My brother Will smiled too, and it was good to see him back in the Alps after nine years.

Those who write off the Breithorn should recognise its ability to make non-climbers feel as though they have just climbed Everest. It was my seventh visit to the summit and it still remained a superb day out. The views are wonderful and the work out is far from negligible, as the round trip is usually about three to four hours. I also realised that each time I had been up there, it had been with different people.

At the summit we did do something different this time. Instead of returning down the normal route we went down the exposed snow slopes across to the Breithorn Central summit (4059m). This was now officially classified as a separate 4000m peak in the new Goedeke guide, and it seemed too good an opportunity to miss. The last part was icy and as a consequence felt harder than we had expected. From this new summit, I looked out along the Breithorn summit ridge and made some mental notes for the future. It looked quite challenging.

The following day, our last of the trip, the four of us walked up to the Hornli Hut. I was pleasantly surprised to find it easy and felt reasonably fit again for the first time in years. It was my first visit for 15 years, and we decided to celebrate with a Rosti on the hut terrace.

After that Will, Ronald and I went to the start of the Hornli Ridge, and did part of the first pitch, so that we could take photographs. We left the next day. James and Hugo's party had no luck as, yet again, and for the rest of the week, it rained in Zermatt, leaving the Matterhorn covered in fresh snow. They did little more than walk forlornly from hut-to-hut.

Weekend Alpinism is an interesting and challenging alternative for those with experience and little time. It breaks all the traditional rules about acclimatisation, but is nonetheless doable and enjoyable if you are fit. The chances of good weather for the two or three days needed are far from good, and we had certainly been lucky over the years. But it was a stopgap driven by the need to balance parenthood, work and budgets.

As I had sat idly watching some climbers returning in triumph from the Matterhorn – this was before the new snow arrived - I vowed to organise a full Alpine trip again in the summer of 2005. It would then be eight years since our last two-week trip in 1997. Most of that time I had struggled with my fitness, so much so that even the middle-ranking Alps had seemed out of reach. The climbs I had done during this period were relatively easy and 'the game' had not felt threatening. I determined to lose weight, get fit and start tackling more serious routes again. But more serious routes would inevitably mean more risk. We didn't know it at the time, but the summer of 2005 would see our 'game' turn deadly.

*'Sadly Richard got the call, just
before the summit.'*

12. Climate change

At the end of December 2004 Agata and I travelled to Kenya to climb Kilimanjaro. Our climbing companions were mainly a group of Polish friends we had met in the Netherlands. Marek and Ania Stawinski were married with two teenage daughters. Gosia Holenderska, a married mum with two grown boys, was also attracted to the adventure. In addition a friend from work, Roger Sexton and his 12-year-old son James, also flew out with us from Heathrow.

On the way we heard the news of the Tsunami, which caused Gosia a good deal of worry as her elder son, Michael was in Phuket at the time. Fortunately, a phone call soon established he was safe.

A few days before we left, I came down, yet again, with flu-like symptoms, which turned into a major throat infection by the time I reached Amsterdam. Fortunately, I was able to get hold of some antibiotics at the airport, but my fever only broke the night before we were due to start climbing the mountain.

We started up the Rongai route and returned through Marangu Gate six days later. It had been a very pleasant trip with good contact with the local guides and porters with whom we celebrated New Year's Eve on the mountain. All of us, except Roger and James had reached Gilmans Point (5681m), whilst Ania and I continued on to Uhuru peak (5895m). I was surprised how strong I felt on the summit, and this filled me with a lot of confidence for the summer ahead.

During the early spring of 2005 I sounded out the others on a new Alpine trip. I pressed for two weeks but Jerry decided not to go. He had met Hilary and they had clicked. Finally, after all those years, his search was at an end, and they were due to get married later that summer. I remembered having made the same decision in 1991 for the same reasons.

In Jerry's place we recruited Nick Martin, a climbing wall friend of James from Brighton and Hugo Hunt, James's brother who had been with us in Zermatt in 2002 and 2004. Hugo is a solicitor from Brighton. Married with a teenage son, he had a great sense of humour and had already climbed in Kazakhstan and the Alps. He and James were incredibly competitive brothers, something that went back half a century or so. Apparently, James had once - by accident - managed to shoot Hugo in the head when they were kids messing about with air pistols. Hugo had never let him forget it, and there was a competition between them to claim the furthest North, South, East or West, along with the highest point reached.

Nick, on the other hand, was an easy-going surfer and one time hang-gliding devotee, who loved the outdoor life and was a walking encyclopaedia on gear. We had never met before but he would effortlessly slot into the team.

'Let's do something completely different this year,' I said to the others.

'What are your ideas?'

'How about starting in the Dauphine? We've never been there and we could do the Barre des Ecrins?'

There was general agreement and we made an ambitious plan. I would drive through the night from the Netherlands and would meet the others in a service station near Lyon at 4.00am. We would then drive to Ailefroide and go straight up to the Glacier Blanc hut (2550m).

The Barre des Ecrins is a Whymper summit and was first climbed in 1864. It is part of the national park and as a consequence has no cable cars. Any ascent is made from the valley floor, the same way as Whymper's original party, whose route we were largely following. This mountain had left a big impression on Whymper and was responsible for a number of classic quotes by the man himself.

'I put it on record as my belief, however sad and however miserable a man may have been, if he is found on the summit of Pointe (Barre) des Ecrins, after a fall of new snow, he is likely to experience misery far deeper than anything which he has hitherto been acquainted.' -Scrambles amongst the Alps – Edward Whymper 1871

Goedeke himself had a few comments, namely that the

Ecrins was a *'profound and fascinating mountain experience'* and that, *'One should not get caught by a storm high on the mountain.'* As this last could be said of any major mountain, we didn't pay too much attention to it at the time.

The potential risks were echoed in another Whymper quote describing his feelings when he found himself caught on the summit ridge.

'Had anyone said to me, "you are a great fool for coming here," I should have answered with humility, "it is true." And had my monitor gone on to say, "swear you will never ascend another mountain if you get down safely," I am inclined to think I should have taken the oath. In fact, the game here was not worth the risk.'- Scrambles amongst the Alps – Edward Whymper 1871

By the time I reached the Glacier Blanc Hut I was feeling in need of some sleep. Hugo, however, had had a far more wretched time. Despite being the fittest guy in the team, he had struggled to find his rhythm after having to return to the car for some crampons. At one stage he had even collapsed and we had been quite worried for a while, but he recovered and powered on up the rest of the way.

The hut itself is solid, pleasant but unremarkable and we all slept well that night. The next morning we were in no particular hurry and had a leisurely breakfast before a late departure up to the Ecrins hut (3170m). The route ahead was quite tricky with some exposed scrambling above a very nasty looking glacier, which at one place even had fixed ropes. It was all a bit harder than we expected, and this day it was my turn to struggle. By the time I finally made it to the Ecrins Hut I was left wondering how fit I really was.

The view from the Ecrins Hut is stunning, with the whole upper part of the Glacier Blanc and the Ecrins summits visible. Even when they occasionally disappeared into cloud there was still a feeling of being somewhere quite special.

During the afternoon we studied the route ahead. This involved an hour's glacier walk in, then a rising and twisting route through the upper glacier, which was adorned with seracs and crevasses, before the summit ridge. The guidebook time was four hours but somehow I knew it would take us longer.

The view was mesmerising and I barely registered as one of the guides at the hut noticed Hugo was carrying a two-way radio and asked him for his frequency,

'Just as a precaution.'

We discussed our plans and decided to get up at 2.00am and leave at 3.00am. This was however vetoed by the hut guardian. He told us that if this was what we really wanted to do we should bivi out, and not wake the rest of the hut who would be waking at 3.00am, setting off at 4.00am.

I remember him as a grizzled old veteran, a guy who would stand no nonsense in his hut, but with a good heart. We heard later how he had insisted on accompanying a climber on a route as they were without a partner and planning to solo.

We were off by 4.00am as intended and headed up the glacier. It was remarkably warm and we could climb without jackets, gloves or hats. After about an hour's snow plodding we heard a huge roar in the distance. It lasted quite a while and I recognised it as an avalanche or serac fall. In fact, on hearing it, one of the guided parties ahead of us turned back.

We saw nothing and continued our upward trek. Within the next hour it became light and it soon became obvious what had happened. A huge serac had fallen across our route; right where we would have been had we set off an hour before. It was dozens of metres wide and had swept away a good 200m of our route. The debris field contained blocks of ice much larger than fridges. Had we left at 3.00am as we had originally intended to, instead of 4.00am we would have been in this zone when the serac collapsed and would have been unlikely to survive the impact from the huge blocks of ice.

It took us 45 minutes to get through this area and by then we were well up the face. The snow slopes were in a poor shape and I noticed that, actually, only half the serac had fallen whilst the other half still hung menacingly above us. We came to a bergshrund, which was already so wide it was barely crossable. In fact we only managed to get across because a small snow ledge remained across the other side from where we - on jumping and landing - could jab our axes into a steep snow slopes and front point up from there.

'Christ, this route won't be do-able within a few days.'

'Yeah or someone will have to bring a ladder.'

Several guided parties turned back there and only a few groups continued with us. Their clients may not have wanted to go on, but it could also be they had been warned about the weather forecast. We knew a storm was forecast for later in the day, but we had no way of knowing that it was moving in more quickly than the forecasters had at first thought.

Above the Bergshrund we traversed below the huge summit ridge of the Barre des Ecrins until we reached just below the Breche Lory. This area bore no relation to the guidebook description, and we were forced up a 25m sixty-degree ice slope. Hugo did a fine lead and, even with protection from above, it felt difficult and loose. We had just about got up this obstacle when the weather began to worsen.

We were at a decision point. A short way along the ridge was the Dome de Neige des Ecrins, now officially a 4000m peak on Goedeke's list. We looked at the Ecrins Ridge and I knew it would take us at least two hours for the five of us to climb the ridge and get back down. At the same time it started snowing and our decision was made, especially as it was James' turn to feel ill.

Fifteen minutes later we were sitting on the summit of the Dome de Neige (4015m.) There was no view of any kind and the photos we took might as well have been taken in a studio, with a white cloth background. As there was little incentive to linger we were gone within minutes.

As we abseiled down the ice gully the snow conditions became a little harder and we started to feel a little hunted. Suddenly the radio, which Hugo was carrying, crackled into life and a voice from the Ecrins Hut called to ask if we were all right. The voice sounded concerned, more than was necessary, even for the conditions we were in. We replied cheerfully that we were fine and continued crossing the bergshrund by jumping down 10ft into the soft snow. Below the bergshrund we emerged from the cloud and soon saw the reason for the radio call.

The other half of the menacing serac had just fallen across

our route. It was even larger than the first and would have had serious consequences had we been under it. Metaphorically it was as if we had just passed between the blades of a revolving propeller. In our own terms we had missed two huge serac falls within hours, and by less than 60 minutes each time. But this was for later analysis. At the time I just dimly registered the facts, put them to the back of my mind, and continued.

There was nothing else we could do anyway but descend the bolder-strewn slopes, yet I was aware that further above us were more dodgy-looking seracs. A few hours earlier I had barely noticed them but now they added to the sense of threat, and I could not rid myself of the thought that if two seracs had already fallen why not these too. The danger zone involved several hundred meters of descent and it would take us 30 minutes or so to descend, even at a fast pace.

We set off in silence and had got about half way down the slope, when there was a huge crack above. For a moment I felt my spine tingle, then the adrenalin cut in and I turned round to see which way I should run, hoping the others would instinctively follow, for we were all roped together. It took several seconds to realise that there was no icefall heading our way, and a few more after that to realise it had been a crack of thunder I had heard.

It was the start of the worst storm to hit the region for many years. We were at about 3400m but within minutes it was raining hard. We had never experienced anything so relentless at this altitude and it would continue all day. After an hour my jacket was soaked and leaking whilst the water seeped down my neck and up my arms from the cuffs of my jacket.

We bypassed the Ecrins Hut but found ourselves descending a difficult glacier with crevasses all around, and some tricky route finding. It was a hard slog, but in a strange way I found it immensely enjoyable despite the discomfort and pervasive anxiety.

Finally we reached the Glacier Blanc Hut, and by now there was not much of me that was still dry even under three layers.

We stopped here for some hot soup and decided to descend to and stay at the Cezanne Hut at the start of the climb rather than try setting up a tent in these conditions. I remembered that Whymper himself had raced to get down the mountain before dark and, having failed, had been forced to bivi out with his favourite guide Croz.

A bivi was unthinkable in our current state and we drove ourselves on to reach the Cezanne Hut by early evening. We left most of our gear outside and settled down in the warmth to a good beer. It continued to rain and storm throughout the night, but by now we were happily ensconced in the bar.

It had been a terrific three days, challenging physically and mentally and a real Alpine adventure. Outwardly we shrugged off the near misses with a few light-hearted comments, for in reality none of us wanted to dwell on it. We were still only at the start of a two-week Alpine climbing trip. 'Surely things must get better from now on,' I thought.

Before the storm we had also seen enough to appreciate the beauty of the Dauphine and its huge potential for climbing, but as the storm was still lingering in the morning, we decided to head further north.

North meant heading to the Valle d'Ayas on the Italian side of the Alps. Again it was new and exciting, and very different from the Dauphine with a classic Northern Italian feel. We settled in Gressoney, where we camped next to a football pitch and managed to hang our still soaking clothes on the goal posts and netting.

We also found a wonderful restaurant near the centre, which lifted our dampened spirits, no end, especially as the first item on the otherwise excellent menu was 'Lamb with herpes'!

'So what are we going to do tomorrow then?'

'It's almost a 1000m climb to the Sella Hut. We can decide there.'

'Let's have a go at the Liskamm West summit.'

'Only if you carry the rope.'

The following day, we took the cable car up to Colle Bettaforca and then climbed up the slopes towards the Sella Hut (3587m). Surprisingly after a few hours the route finding became a little tricky and the final part was on a somewhat exposed ridge with fixed ropes. It was both fun and unexpected and we reached the hut in high spirits.

No sooner had we arrived than the weather started to deteriorate, something we all pretended to ignore. The hut guardian filled us in on conditions above and we repaired to a table to have a good chat about our next day's objectives. Initially we had intended to go for the Liskamm West Face. This was described by Goedeke as *'one of the highest technically less difficult Alpine summits'* and was graded PD.

This was one of the new additions to the guidebook, as the West summit was now defined as being on a par with the East summit. The Liskamm has a dangerous reputation and we were wary on hearing from the hut guardian that its west ridge route was badly iced up and in poor condition.

We did have an alternative, which was to climb up the Felixhorn, and from there along the South East Ridge of Castor (4228m) also graded PD. We had climbed Castor back in 1994 but then it had been from the Kleine Matterhorn. So, although the summit would not be new, the route would be. I favoured Castor and JR favoured the Liskamm with the others undecided. The matter was left until morning.

That night a storm blew up and threatened to make our route discussions irrelevant. I remember lying in the hut listening to the wind howling across the roof with huge force, wondering idly what I would grab first if the roof indeed blew off. We decided to delay our departure and the hours dragged by. I drifted back to sleep feeling guilty about my lack of drive to get going.

Then at 8.00am JR woke us.

'Come on guys, I think the weather has improved.'

'Huhhh.'

'Other people are setting off too. Come on we can still do this. Get your arses in gear.'

Within half an hour we set off into a still howling wind. The skies cleared as we moved up the slopes of the Felik glacier but the wind, if anything, got worse. By the time we reached the decision point at the Felikjoch, JR agreed to go for Castor.

We followed an attractive series of ridges, passed the

Felixhorn (4174m) a minor 4000m summit and walked along towards the main summit of Castor. The ridge was exposed and we estimated the wind at about 100km/hour. No real communication was possible and we plodded on, lost in our own worlds, just mechanically following the rope and the person in front. Had I been alone I would probably have turned back but here there was no chance of even discussing it. The final ridge looked horribly steep and narrow but I switched off my mind and set off up it.

This ability to switch off has always been useful in these types of situations, where confidence in one's ability was at a premium. The wind was stinging and bitterly cold and every bit of exposed skin felt burned. The summit was small, far smaller than I could remember, and we could barely fit the five of us on. I just had time to look along the ridge down towards Pollux, take one photo, and we were off back down.

By now, James had lost the feeling in the fingers of one hand and the cloud had come in. With every stitch of clothing on, we could do little but tell him to try and warm it in his pocket and it took us an hour to get back to the Felikjoch, where we were out of the worst of the wind. Fortunately James had managed to avoid any serious damage to his fingers although they were numb at the ends for some time after.

As we descended back to the valley floor, the weather started to improve. That evening, we analysed the day's events in our favourite restaurant.

'Why are we getting hit by bad weather all the time?'

'It's called climate change. Did you know banks won't lend money to ski resorts below 1500m any more?'

'It's not just the storms. There have always been storms. It's the warming.'

'Yeah, remember that morning of the Ecrins. We could have been wearing T shirts.'

'I don't like it. It's making this game a lot more dangerous.'

We talked about a lot of other things that night. Nick had an endless line of stories, most including women, and he lowered the tone to exactly the right level. By now I was feeling the effects of having spent five out of the last six days climbing and the other day driving. I desperately wanted a rest day, but the next morning we packed up and headed for Switzerland.

We considered Chamonix but in the end we went to Saas Grund. James and JR were keen to have a go at the Nadelhorn and felt no need for a rest day. I had decided not to go with them as I felt quite exhausted and Nick also wanted a rest. Hugo decided to stay with us too and so I dropped James and JR off up at Saas Fee the next morning for their climb up to the Mischabel Hut.

Again the weather forecast was poor with yet another storm forecast for the next day. We decided, however, to have a go at climbing the Allalinhorn, which neither Nick nor Hugo had climbed before and which I had no objections to doing again.

Early next morning we set off for the first cable car, and then caught the train up to the MittelAllalin. It was a repeat of the Barre des Ecrins all over again, and we reached the summit in thick cloud and snow with a major storm coming in. We descended without incident and were sitting in Saas Fee drinking a beer and watching the rain falling when we saw James and JR walking by.

They were tired and in a state of mild shock. Having reached the Mischabel Hut the day before, they had set out early that morning for the Nadelhorn. This involved crossing the Hohbalmgletscher and the conditions had been awful. A thin insubstantial layer of snow had covered the crevasses, the kind of classic glacier conditions that are the stuff of nightmares where every step could mean dropping through into a huge chasm. Both had indeed fallen into crevasses and watched others do the same.

'Almost everyone on that glacier went in at one stage.' explained JR.

'It was quite interesting.' said James, which in plain English meant 'desperate'.

'One guy went right in and was hanging on the rope stuck under a roof of snow and ice.'

"Yeah, took ages for him to get out. He kept shouting 'stop pulling' to his mates, as he was stuck under this ledge of ice and being pulled up against it with his head!"

'He got out by using his ice axe on it and hacking a hole.'

Most parties had turned back after this, but James and JR, along with another British party, had continued on. Half way up the final ridge, however, the storm started to get worse and, as there was also rock climbing to do on the very exposed ridge, the lads had decided to retreat. Now they were wondering, beer in hand, if they should have gone on. James, in particular, was haunted by the thought of having given in too soon, but in my opinion, they had certainly made the right decision.

Now back in the safety of Saas Fee they were feeling the effects of their epic and we drank a fair bit of beer that afternoon. It seemed not only was bad weather following us but also the gods were trying to tell us something.

The poor weather left us disinclined to stay in Saas Grund and we decided to make for Chamonix. Early in the holiday James had still hoped we might want to have a go at the Matterhorn with him, but he now accepted this was not going to happen. The 'Big M' was not a mountain to be attempted in the kind of weather conditions we had been experiencing.

In Chamonix we found the Molliasses campsite shut for renovation. It was not clear what this involved, as everything from the outside looked the same as before, so we guessed it must be safety work higher up the slopes. We found an alternative and walked into Chamonix and the Jeckyl bar.

For the next few days we remained in the bars as it continued to rain. I remember discussing Tony Blair's recent third election victory and was surprised how 'anti' my friends had become. It made me realise how much out of touch I had become by living abroad.

We saw Nick off at the station as his holiday time had run out. He had been fun to be with and I hoped he would be up for more climbing trips in the future. It was also around this time we managed to play an excellent practical joke on James. After a meal in the only Indian restaurant in Chamonix, James had gone to sleep with his head tilted back and mouth wide open. We managed to place Nan bread on his head and a piece of lemon in his mouth without him waking up and then took a photograph.

He has been threatening revenge ever since. James' outrage was softened however by the news that 'le grand beau temps' was about to appear at last.

We had long debated our next move. I wanted to climb the Cosmique Arête on the Aiguille du Midi and Hugo was keen to go along. It was a short classic rock climb with a wonderfully exposed finish. We also wanted to climb Mont Maudit, also known as the 'accursed mountain', which is situated almost midway between Mont Blanc du Tacul and Mont Blanc itself.

Mont Maudit had surprisingly been ignored by parties climbing Mont Blanc for a hundred years before falling to another Anglo-Swiss team in 1878. The principal dangers lay in the weather as it was along way from home.

After some discussion, it was decided that Hugo and I would do the Aiguille du Midi first then go for Mont Maudit the next day, something which involved climbing the North West Face of Mont Blanc du Tacul, which we had climbed back in 1997. It had snowed quite a bit recently and we all agreed that because of the avalanche risk, we should leave the Tacul slopes to consolidate for another day.

Hugo and I discussed matters and decided to do what we had never done before and get a guide for the route. I reasoned that it should be part of one's Alpine climbing experience at least once.

As the weather improved we got to see some of the other people in the campsite. Next to us were a Dutch couple and opposite us were six young British climbers, with military haircuts and a large van. It seemed that everyone was looking forward to getting to grips with the mountains again.

Hugo and I met our guide at the Midi cable car and descended to the start of the route which goes up the South West side of the Aiguille du Midi. The route is a classic with a move of grade IV and a lot of grade III rock climbing. The weather was superb and for the first time on the holiday we enjoyed a wide view of our surroundings. Stunning is an understatement and we could not keep our eyes off it, whilst the airy finish up to the terraces of the Midi is a memorable one.

A few hours later we were back in the campsite chatting to the others in the sun, when suddenly there was a major commotion. One helicopter after another began landing at the Mountain Rescue base a few hundred metres from our campsite and it was clear that a significant rescue effort was underway.

As we were cooking in the campsite later that evening we noticed that one of the British climbers opposite us had returned but was walking around in a daze. JR approached him and learned the story. They were part of a British Army team who had been hit by a massive serac fall while descending the slopes of the North West Face of Mt Blanc du Tacul. The ice caught five out of six and all had been airlifted out. One was dead on arrival in Chamonix. Three more were seriously injured remained in hospital.

This tragedy happened less than an hour after Hugo and I had completed the Cosmique Arête, overlooking the North West Face and the helicopters we had seen were for our campsite neighbours. It was a grim fact that we had taken photographs of the North West Face as we had finished the route, and these would show the large serac less than sixty minutes before its collapse.

The young survivor was walking around the van in a state of shock, but he refused any help. We were outsiders and he wouldn't let us in. The army would deal with this in private.

The next morning an officer arrived to help the young lad and the van was soon gone. We heard later it was a Captain who had been the one killed and I remembered seeing him the day before making preparations.

We sat on our campsite chairs and discussed things over breakfast. The local newspaper had the story on its front page and a colour photograph showed a huge serac fall, which had fanned some 300 metres across the face.

It crossed my mind that had we gone for the Mont Maudit the same day instead of waiting, we too might have been caught in this serac collapse as our route went the same way and we would have been in that region at the same time.

What also preyed on my mind was that only half the serac

had fallen and the other half hung menacingly over the face, in a disturbing repeat of our Barre des Ecrins experience. This had warned us not go the day before, but now I discovered the others were still keen to have a go at Mont Maudit.

'But what about the serac still there, it could come down at any time?'

'I know but we've been taking these kinds of risks all holiday.'

'But you'll also be returning that way in the midday sun, prime risk time.'

'What if we traverse Mont Blanc and come down the Gouter Ridge?'

'That's a hell of a long way though.'

'I'd rather do that, though, than return down that face in the sun. We would be in the danger zone for a long time – for at least an hour.'

'It should be alright at four in the morning though.'

The others were determined to go and having had my way the previous day I could hardly complain. We packed our kit and set off for the now familiar Midi cable car. I must admit to feeling a distinct lack of enthusiasm and wondered what kind of people we had become, that we would go up the same slopes a day after this tragedy. We were no longer wild young men but middle aged with families. Whatever the answer, though, we were not alone, as dozens of climbers could be found queuing for tickets.

We again descended the steep ridge that led from the Midi to the Cosmique Hut and caught sight of the remains of the serac.

'My God, it's massive.'

'Look what's still left up there though.'

Above the slope hung another huge serac, which had clearly been attached to the fallen ice just the day before. It looked overhanging and just a sneeze at the wrong moment might set it off.

I was mesmerized by the slopes above and began to find dangers, which I had never seen before as every crevasse or slope suddenly felt threatening. Goedeke had warned that this face was potentially dangerous and *'threatened by infrequent but unpredictable serac avalanches.'*

That evening I worked things through in my mind. If we did Mont Maudit only and returned back the same way there was no way of avoiding a long descent in the sun under the serac in question. On the other hand I doubted I was fit enough to traverse Mont Blanc despite my acclimatisation. These were the only two realistic options and neither was appealing. And I considered my position as a father with a lovely four-year-old daughter whose birthday was due within a week.

I announced to the others that I had decided not to go in the morning.

'Look guys, I don't mind going up the face early in the morning, but I'm not returning that way in the midday sun and I'm simply not fit enough to traverse Mont Blanc. Plus tomorrow is my last day and I have to drive to Dortmund the day after tomorrow by myself to meet Agata and Katie at the airport there.'

It was the first time in my life I had declined to do a route my mates were doing on the basis that it was too dangerous. Another first, but I was not being critical of the others. They were not planning to return down the slopes at midday either, but being fitter were simply more confident of being able to complete a traverse of Mont Blanc. As it turned out we all made the right decision.

At three o'clock in the morning we woke along with the fifty or so others in the hut. I joined the lads for breakfast as a gesture to team morale, but had not changed my mind. The others disappeared before 4.00am and I went back to sleep. Then a few hours after dawn I sneaked out and made my way back up to the Midi cable car.

That day I kept in touch with the others by mobile phone, and charted their progress. The first call confirmed they had climbed Mont Maudit by the North East Ridge. At the col before the final slopes of Mont Blanc they had rested a good while before summiting late morning.

From here it was all down hill along the same route I had followed with Tony and Terrence seventeen years earlier. They had an hour's rest at the Gouter Hut, and then set off down.

I was waiting with drinks and snacks when they finally hove into view at the car park at Les Houches. They looked weary but pleased and had a legion of stories to tell. It had been a superb performance.

'Did you know the local authorities are claiming 30% of those returning from Mont Blanc are injured with frostbite, AMS or wounds from crampons?'

'James has got a sore toe, does that count?'

'My knees are a bit sore too.'

'Shame, I didn't see anyone counting today. That might skew the figures a bit.'

We spent our last evening in the Jeckyl Bar, in a quiet, thoughtful mood. We had been through two adventurous weeks with hardly a difference of opinion between us and despite the poor weather had managed to climb a good number of summits. In truth, though, I felt somewhat traumatized by the dangers and near misses, which we had experienced. Could I really justify this? 'Not really,' I admitted to myself for the first time. The depth of this feeling was new and disturbing. Nor was it my only worry.

My love for the Alps remained but during our climbs that summer we had seen plenty of evidence of the effects of climate change. Retreating glaciers with rivers of melt water, rock fall and collapsing seracs were becoming more common. It was also warmer at 4.00am above 3200m than I had ever experienced and bergshrunds were becoming impassable earlier in the season. Crevasse fields were also becoming more dangerous and the rocks seemed to becoming looser. The ramifications go far wider, and we are unlikely to reverse this change in our lifetime and need to take action to avoid things getting a whole lot worse for our children.

Normally, my return to work after a holiday like this was difficult, but now I felt enthused. My work at Philips involved promoting energy efficient lighting solutions as an important solution to reducing our energy consumption, and indirectly reducing, the increase in our carbon emissions.

We were going to lobby in Brussels for more awareness of the need to switch from older lighting to the latest technologies. A global switch, we had calculated, would save more than 550 million tonnes of CO_2 and 100 billion Euros in electricity costs per year. I was paid to do this, of course, but it also came from the heart. Preserving the Alpine regions, as far as this is possible, was a powerful motivator.

Meanwhile, climate change would continue to have its consequences. I did not yet know it, but the next time I would play 'the game' it would coincide with an all time record accident rate.

'In which James learned about the dangers
of falling asleep in an Alpine curry house.'

13. The 'young lady' at last

It was two years before I was ready to face climbing in the Alps again. Psychologically I needed to get away from it all for a while, and during this time my climbing books lay collecting dust. Seeking new challenges I threw myself into other projects, of which, fortunately, I had plenty.

In the late summer of 2005, we attended Jerry and Hilary's wedding in North London. It was a Jewish wedding, which Agata and I had never experienced before, and it was really good to see our old mate getting hitched after all these years. There was a lot of fun and dancing, although a fair number of people, including myself, were also following England's Ashes-winning progress in the test match via mobile phones and SMS text messages.

That autumn I was busy for my work promoting energy efficient lighting. We held a press event in Brussels in October and had an enthusiastic response. This work continued into 2006, with numerous events and the creation of new partnerships with pan-European organisations. At the end of 2006, Philips called for incandescent light bulbs to be phased out, and we put our case to the highest levels in governments all around Europe. It was stimulating work, which really felt worthwhile.

During the winter of 2005/6, I became fascinated by stories of the early Victorian African explorers. Books on Livingstone, Burton, Speke and Stanley kept me awake late into the winter nights as the search for the source of the Nile came alive. I put forward the idea of another African trip in the summer to Agata and our Polish friends.

Then in late May 2006 Agata and I, along with Will, Gosia and Ilse, a friend from work, walked the Hadrian's Wall trail in six days. It was a nice week and one of my main memories was my brother, yet again turning up without a raincoat. The weather had been awful and the forecast was bad but this had not worried

Will. In fact, he was incredibly lucky as we had only one rain shower all week. Some things never change.

By the summer of 2006 our African trip had also been sorted out. It was agreed that we would climb Mt Kenya and then go to the source of the Nile in Uganda. We were an international group. Marek and Ania joined us again with their two teenage daughters Karolina and Magdalena. We also had a Russian woman friend called Angelica who spoke no English, Dutch or Polish and with whom only Ania could communicate. Both Roger and James joined us as well.

We spent an adventurous week climbing Mount Kenya, Point Lenana (4895m) and traversing down the Chogoria route. Uganda too was an interesting place to visit and we ended taking the old Nairobi-Mombasa overnight railway to the coast at the end of the trip.

On our return, we decided as a group to sponsor Enock, one of our Kilimanjaro porters, through college. This, in turn, led me to set up a 'Save the snow' initiative, in which 45 colleagues and their families from work would climb Kilimanjaro at the end of 2007. We had two aims. Firstly to raise awareness for the need for a switch to energy efficient lighting and secondly to raise a large amount of money for an Oxfam Novib water irrigation project in Tanzania, which had a clear link to climate change.

In the late summer of 2006 our son Michael life went in a new direction, when he moved to Dublin with his current girl friend. He had only studied for a year in the US before deciding to return home. Subsequently he had started courses in Maastricht and Eindhoven, but was now ready for the world of work.

The winter of 2006/7 was busy from a work point of view. We prepared for the Al Gore 'Live Earth' concerts, as climate change became a mainstream issue. Philips was a sponsor and I again helped organise an international press event to promote energy efficient lighting. Agata and I went to the Wembley concert and I realised that a lot of the audience hadn't even been born at the time of Bob Geldof's Live Aid concert 22 years before.

It was early summer 2007 before my thoughts turned again seriously to the Alps. By now my doubts had been suppressed to the extent that I could contemplate another serious Alpine effort. I lost a good deal of weight and got into training again.

Putting the team together proved surprisingly easy. James was very keen as usual and JR also decided to come. Nick Martin could do a week, whilst my brother Will decided to join us at the start for a long weekend. Out of the blue, my old friend Mark Phillips decided to come along too. I had not climbed with Mark since the Eiger some seventeen years before, but he had recently divorced and now had more time on his hands. Then we learned that Richard, Ana-Maria and their boys were planning to spend a few weeks in Grindelwald. Plans were made to do a route with Richard somewhere during his holiday.

There were some no shows too. Neither Hugo, who was planning a trip to Nepal to climb a 7000m peak, nor Jerry, who was temporarily without a job and living the life of a kept man, could join us.

Agata and Katie were due to go to Poland for three weeks in mid July 2007 and I planned my own precious time carefully. I was determined to spend some time relaxing in Zermatt first, which I knew would not be to everyone's liking. I therefore decided to go out midweek, four days before James, JR and Mark would arrive. It would also allow me to acclimatise properly for once rather than go charging straight up a 4000m peak - subconsciously I still needed to ease my way back into Alpinism after the traumatic events of Chamonix two years earlier.

I wanted to climb the Jungfrau (4158m) as it would mean completing the famous Oberland trio and finally achieve what I had vowed to do more than two decades earlier. In order to do this, however, I was determined not to rush up un-acclimatised. This time I would do things 'by the book.' Then, two weeks before we were due to go, someone showed me a news item on the BBC news website. An avalanche on the normal route of the Jungfrau - the very route I was planning to take, had just killed six Swiss climbers. Suddenly it felt like 2005 all over again.

Both Nick Martin and Brother Will liked the idea of a trip to Zermatt and agreed to join me. We had a fun, relaxing few days, helped by another vintage Will performance. He arrived at Zermatt campsite carrying a whole load of impractical - even useless - things such as a kids table and chairs set and a disposable BBQ. He had neglected to bring a rucksack and carried everything else in plastic Tesco bags, which made him a sight to behold. I was immediately suspicious and soon discovered he had not brought a jacket.

'Yeeaah I know. I couldn't find it in my cupboard, but I brought three fleeces,' he added cheerfully.

Nick and I marched him straight down to the first climbing gear shop we came across and made him get his credit card out. Even so, I couldn't help but laugh.

'Will, you're 35 now, and you're not walking round a park in London. This is the Alps!'

'I'll be all right. This really is an excellent new jacket, you know.'

Will was very fit having just run his third London Marathon a few months earlier, and I was determined to let him carry the heavy gear this time. On our first day we walked along the Gornergrat Ridge from Rotenboden (2813m) to the Stockhorn (3405m), which took longer than we expected, even though Will was carrying our extensive picnic. On the way back we caught a close up of an Ibex in classic pose, silhouetted on a ridge against the background of Monte Rosa.

A storm was forecast for the afternoon of our second day, so we went for a walk up the valley towards the Schwarzee, following paths through fields I had never visited. We passed wooden huts, which Whymper would have recognised, and stopped for drinks at cafes, laughing at Nick's endless stories, and some of the eccentric characters we came across. We returned down beautiful forest trails below the Riffelalp, where I had last walked with Terrence twenty years before. It was tranquil and just what I needed before the bigger experiences which I knew were bound to follow.

That afternoon in the rain, I wandered around Zermatt

looking at the places I had been to over the years. Everywhere there were tourists, enticed by a huge range of activities. Surely now a limit on numbers must have been reached.

It was all superb therapy. In the evenings we visited our favourite places, the North Wall Bar, and Whymper's 'Pad', amongst others. I had a good chat with Will, the best for many years. He was now working for the London Stock Exchange but was feeling unchallenged by the relaxed pace he found there.

I also came to realise how much Nick too had been affected by our trip two years before and how he had been outside his comfort zone. 'If I were to die in the mountains I'd be really really pissed off,' he told me one day.

For the first time, I found it difficult to sleep in Zermatt campsite. The trains and other nocturnal sounds woke me time after time. This in itself was strange as normally I was a good sleeper.

We visited the excellent new underground Alpine museum in the centre of town. Besides the famous severed Whymper rope, which I had seen many times before, I found a letter from a young Winston Churchill describing his ascent of Monte Rosa in 1892.

On the third day we climbed the Breithorn in the classic way – that is in poor weather and by taking the cable car to the Kleine Matterhorn. Here again there was strong evidence of climate change, as the tunnel entrance onto the glacier now needed steps because of reduced snow depth.

We arrived back from the Breithorn, and had been lying in the sun for only a few hours when the others arrived. I knew the moment I saw them all striding purposefully towards us that our relaxed pace was about to change. James, JR and Mark were understandably bursting with energy, and keen to get to grips with the Alps. Maps appeared along with guidebooks and ambitious plans were made, most of which involved a non-stop enchainment of 4000m peaks, and assumed perfect fitness and weather. After a while it was decided to continue the discussion in a Zermatt hostelry.

I remained in the tent. My lack of sleep left me feeling both disinterested and older. It was an odd feeling, which I had never experienced before, and it took me until the evening before I could join in the discussions.

We climbed the Riffelhorn (2927m) next day. This is generally seen as good practice, having a large number of rock climbs in a superb setting. James and Mark went up it first, taking a route round the back, on the face opposite the Breithorn's North Wall, and wearing rock boots. Nick, JR and I followed on a separate rope and we were very slow. We had no rock boots or guidebook, but had a general idea of the route, which Nick led.

It made a nice change to be on rock again rather than softening snow, and without a guidebook there was a feeling of pioneering up the route. The summit was in full sunshine and we had a long debate about which summit was actually the highest. From one point the other looked clearly lower but when we scrambled across to the other we had the opposite impression.

Our descent was just as slow as the ascent. We over-insured every abseil and did nothing without a general discussion, and a three-way check of everything. By the time we had got back down to the lake, it was late afternoon and time to descend. It had been good practice, but I realised that my body was no longer capable of doing what it could two decades before. It was another reminder of the ageing process. However, this little adventure did speed up our rope work for the rest of the holiday.

The following day, the mood in our camp was not as light as the day before. A number of factors accounted for this. The forecast for the next few days was poor with a major storm due. JR was feeling rather off colour with flu-like symptoms and James and Mark had burned off a lot of energy going up the Gornergrat ridge, after the Riffelhorn, with very heavy sacks.

I suggested another acclimatisation walk. With the storm due by early afternoon it was the only sensible thing to do. We selected the Oberothorn (3415m) and spent a few hours up at the Rothorn paradise area of Zermatt, which I had never been to before. From here we had a grandstand view of the incoming weather front, moving up from Italy. The storm broke before we got back to the tents and it rained heavily for the rest of the day and night.

By now, even I had had enough of Zermatt and its rain. We decided to move out to the Oberland the next day.

That evening I pondered the changes I had witnessed in Zermatt in the last twenty years. It seemed busier still and the numbers of battery driven vehicles, which were needed to maintain everything, was stretching the ethic of no cars on the streets. The marketing though was superb and I still admired the business acumen and creativity of the locals who had utilised almost every bit of land they had.

We piled our gear and ourselves into my car at the new multi story car park at Tasch, and drove round to Grindelwald. It rained for a good deal of the way but then cleared up as we approached our destination. We had major plans. There would be no setting up tents and drying things out. We were going to go straight up to the Jungfraujoch, itself now a UNESCO World Heritage Site, and from there to the Mönch Hut.

On the way we passed the Eiger glacier station and Mark and I reflected on our last visit here in 1990. I had heard that virtually no one climbed the Eiger West Face route any more due to the loose rock. The preference now was for the Mittelegi Ridge, or the South Ridge. On the train up the girl collecting the tickets was concerned to hear we were going climbing. There had been a lot of accidents recently she told us.

Walking from the top station to the Mönch Hut it started snowing – and this would continue most of the evening. The hut itself looked just as we had left it twelve years before, although Jerry's favourite Swiss girl was long gone

'She's probably running a division of a major Swiss multinational.'

'Or a big name global charity.'

'She might have chosen to have six kids instead.'

'She might be doing both.'

We checked in and found ourselves at the dinner table with Steve Bell - the proprietor of Jagged Globe, a climbing and trekking company based in Sheffield, who was guiding. Everest guide Kenton Cool was at the next table and we joked that all we needed now was Martin Moran to complete the trio.

Because of the heavy snowfall, we decided to avoid the Jungfrau and warm up instead on the Mönch. This was the same route we had done in 1995 and I remembered the exposed ridge we had crossed then. One advantage of the Mönch was that it did not require a very early start, but we were keen and it was still dark when we set off. The weather had cleared but it became obvious that the heavy snowfall had turned the mountain into a very different proposition than 12 years earlier. Deep soft snow forced us onto the sides of the ridge where there was little natural protection. The climbing felt precarious and I was relieved when we reached the ridge proper higher up the route.

From here we made steady progress but I never felt comfortable on the loose powder snow. Just after dawn, when we were half way up the route, there was a sudden commotion. The calm of the mountains was broken by the noise of a rescue helicopter, which started hovering over the summit area of the Mönch itself. The chopper hung around for quite a while before darting off to the valley. We heard later a major rescue operation had been underway for six climbers who had got stuck on the South West Ridge overnight and who were suffering from exposure. They had been close to death.

As we reached the start of the final ridge, I took my glove off to take a photo of Mark, who was leading, and accidentally dropped it. It fluttered down the face and had Mark not been carrying a spare I would probably have had to descend. It was a small detail to carry a spare glove on these climbs, and for many years I always had, but complacency had set in. It's small things like this, which matter in the Alps.

About this time, Steve Bell and his client came down past us. I asked them about the ridge ahead.

'It's not too bad. The snow is good, but there's one bit, which is very exposed, and you'll want to be on a tight rope.'

The ridge was pretty much as it had been in 1995, that is to say, sensationally exposed with steep drops on both sides, and one always had a feeling of being on a cornice. Disturbingly I had several visions of my daughter Katie during this traverse, something that had never happened before.

We soon reached the area that Steve Bell had referred to. It was another 'switch off your brain' moment! The ridge narrowed to a foot wide with 50-degree snow and ice slopes dropping out of sight directly below, on both sides. It was like walking across the ridge tiles of a roof but one, which dropped half a mile on either side. Being tied to my companions, there was nothing to do except continue, and shortly after we reached the summit. This was smaller than I remembered and about ten climbers were already there. This left no place to sit and we merely huddled together, as each rope sorted itself out for the descent.

I could sense a monstrous traffic jam coming up, as we could see many more parties below approaching the summit ridge, and we decided to set off back immediately.

Half way back across the ridge we started to meet the other parties and we had the delicate job of passing each other. This was done invariably with good humour. It crossed my mind that it would be a miracle if there were no accidents this day. The conditions were simply dangerous.

Our descent of the lower ridge involved one long traffic jam with climbers coming up and down. This greatly spoiled the pleasure of the day, and it was early afternoon before we had safely reached the bottom of the route.

Once down, we all lay down in the sun to rest and reflect. JR was still not feeling well, whilst James looked indifferent to the whole experience and complained that the traffic jams had ruined his day. Mark, who had carried a lot of the burden of leading, was strangely quiet and suddenly began being sick. Worried that his puke was bright red, it took us a minute to realise he was throwing up his 'Marsch thee', the special tea offered to climbers at the hut for their water bottles, and was not suffering from some serious internal bleeding.

I thought about the views I had seen. Years earlier I had declared the view from the Mönch as the best I had ever seen in the Alps. A few days earlier on the Riffelhorn, I had begun to doubt this judgement on witnessing a 360-degree panorama of the Matterdal up close. Now I had reverted to my previous view and still think the view from the Mönch, on a clear day, is the finest Alpine view I have ever witnessed. Its grandeur lies in its reach, for not only can you see 360 degrees but it has both close ups and distant views, with the Matterhorn too being clearly visible.

Back at the Hut, Mark went straight to his bunk where he remained for the rest of the day. James, JR and I discussed what to do next. I was still determined to attempt the Jungfrau but knew that the recent snowfalls would have made it more prone to avalanche. James, too, was up for it but JR said he needed to rest a day to recover fully. As always we soon reached a happy compromise, where we would remain at the hut, have a rest day and then go for the Jungfrau the day after. This would allow JR to rest and the snow slopes to consolidate.

That evening a large mixed group of British Army climbers arrived at the hut. One of the young officers quizzed me on conditions above, and I shared what I could. I mentioned our experiences with their colleagues in Chamonix two years earlier and he acknowledged knowing about the incident. I realised looking at him that he was about half my age, and that I must appear an old man!

The following day, we got up late and wandered down to the Jungfraujoch. Mark announced he would descend as he was still suffering from altitude. This left three of us to tackle the route the next day. We had lunch in the restaurant and watched distant climbers coming back down the South East Ridge of the Jungfrau. Disturbingly there were also still clear traces of the huge avalanche, which had recently killed the six Swiss climbers. A close study of the route revealed many more potential dangers and it took a continuous effort not to dwell on it.

I knew I didn't have to attempt the Jungfrau at all. I could descend right now and drive anywhere I wanted, without having to feel any shame. But the impulse to go on was simply stronger.

I had declared it my main aim, and this meant in my mind that I was committed. Looking at James and JR I drew comfort from being with good, experienced friends.

The Jungfrau (4158m) is a truly beautiful mountain and is the third highest peak in the Bernese Alps. Legend says it was named after the young nuns of Interlaken, who used to maintain pastures on Wengeneralp in centuries gone by.

It was climbed for the first time in 1811 by two brothers Johann Rudolf Meyer and Hieronymus along with the Chamois hunters Alos Volker and Joseph Bortis in a four-day expedition during the early days of Alpinism. Ironically they had not been believed and repeated the climb the following year with a flag. Even then there were doubters.

I knew from John and Liz, who had climbed it in 1992, that the top part was quite tricky. Goedeke too was hardly encouraging. He described it as '*a peak with a high accident rate*' and warned of '*constant crevasse danger*' and '*dangerous snow conditions in the second half of the day*'. On the positive side he did allow it that it had '*Magnificent views*'. It was graded PD+.

That evening we learned that yet another storm was due later the following day. This was disturbing news and left us scratching our heads. Then as we sat down for our evening meal, Martin Moran and a few clients suddenly joined us. We had a good chat with them, for they had just completed the Nollen route on the Mönch and were intending to have a go at the Gross Fiescherhorn the next day. We shared information on routes and recent weather and snow conditions. I found myself re-energised by such company.

This was just as well for at 4.00am the following morning, just before we were due for breakfast, James reported it was blowing a gale outside. This was crisis time, and all my senses told me to go back to bed and sleep. It was dark outside; we had barely slept at all and were heading for a dangerous mountain, with a major storm due later, although, judging by the sound of the wind it might already have arrived.

I watched from our breakfast table, as even Martin Moran seemed to be having doubts. We sat drinking tea and making desultory conversation, but all the time searching for clues about how we all felt.

In such circumstances it takes strength not to give in, but from somewhere we now found this strength. Deep down, all three of us really wanted to have a go at this mountain, and we had waited long enough.

'Why don't we set off and see how it goes? We can always return if it's no good.'

'Yeah let's make a final decision when we reach the rock band. It should be light by then.'

'I'm up for it,' said James.

It constantly amazed me how keen James was, despite his age, to continue playing 'the game.' I always had a feeling that if I had called out: 'who wants to try the North Face of the Eiger in winter?' James would say, 'I'm up for it.' His inherent confidence and fearlessness was a great boost.

We set off just before dawn, and raced down the slopes towards the key rock band at the start of the route proper. By the time we were there, it was apparent that we had made the right decision, because the wind had dropped and a clear dawn was emerging. We scrambled through the rock band, which involved some grade II rock climbing, and which was quite exposed in parts.

Above this, we trudged up the steepening snow slopes towards the Rottalsattel and, on stopping for a Mars Bar, found ourselves surrounded by birds that came very close, hoping for a titbit. A few hours later we passed under the threatening slopes of the Rottalhorn, and arrived at the bergshrund below the Rottalsattel. This involved 25m of climbing up softening snow on a 50-60 degree headwall, and onto an exposed ridge.

The last 350m of the Jungfrau are the trickiest and most dangerous. This is also where many accidents have occurred. It involved climbing a steep snow slope, which had drops on both sides. The main problem, we found, was that the snow was soft. Iron stakes had been placed up the side of the ridge and we used these wherever we could. In places, the angle of the slope felt like 50 degrees.

After 200m or so, the angle eased slightly. We were totally alone in this white world, a complete contrast to the Mönch. The summit region was attractive and offered easy scrambling after which a short ridge brought us to the summit. I was pleased to see that despite the conditions we had done it in less than five hours, within guidebook time.

The summit was quite small and just accommodated the three of us. I got a great view of the Eiger West Face and the Mönch South East Ridge, all in one background. The weather was still reasonably clear and the storm was not yet in sight. We shook hands I had a sneaking thought that we had made it despite everything, but we had too many dangers to face on the return for me to relax yet. The steep slopes up which we had come were softening by the minute and I felt a need to get down as quick as possible.

So after five minutes we were off again. Despite the stanchions it was hard work and the snow only just firm enough to hold us. Another half an hour and I doubt I would have managed it without slipping. During this descent I had several more visions of my daughter Katie – just visual images flashing through my mind. We worked our way back to the Rottalsattel where I protected JR as he down climbed a steep 25m section. James was last down, unprotected from above and facing a full rope length fall if he came off. I watched him carefully but he seemed completely unperturbed.

It was remarkable how soft the snow was becoming. It was only late morning and we had seen little sun, but already an ascent in these conditions would be unthinkable. The lower we got the worse the snow became. In the last part above the rock step we were often sinking in thigh deep, and this made our descent even more tiring than our ascent a few hours earlier.

We abseiled down the rock step and finally sat at the start of the glacier re-ascent to the Jungfraujoch. Here we rested and then roped up. JR volunteered to lead.

'For Christ's sake, don't fall in a crevasse now.' I laughed at him.

'No chance,' he replied, 'I'm looking forward to a cold beer.'

We estimated that it would be about an hour and a half to get back in these conditions. By now it was clear that bad weather was imminent and the clouds were darkening by the minute. Fortunately the glacier had a trail and we were able to make steady progress. After 20 minutes, I had reached the trance state where your mind is on autopilot when suddenly I saw JR who was 25m ahead of me almost disappear from view.

He was up to his shoulders in a crevasse and I instinctively dived onto my axe. I shouted to James to come up and help, but although there was only 25m between us, it took him more than a minute in the soft snow. JR was clearly wrestling with the crevasse up front and I could only see his head and shoulders sticking out of the glacier. It took him a minute to extricate himself and another minute to recover. He had been fortunate to become wedged at the shoulders, which stopped him plunging right through.

We shouted encouragements and made rude gestures to cheer him up, but he seemed unaffected and warned us to make a detour. As we past we could see a nasty looking crevasse, still half hidden by the snow. From then on we were at full alert – it was one thing to know that the glacier contained crevasses but when you have seen a mate fall in it becomes far more immediate.

A glacier in these circumstances is a lottery and after another ten minutes I suddenly felt my legs collapsing into a hole below me. Instinctively I threw myself forward across the gap and jammed my ice axe into the other side. A nasty deep looking crevasse appeared below my legs but fortunately I had enough purchase on my axe not to fall through any further.

James had seen me go and I was on a tight rope. I scrambled up and away from the immediate danger. We continued but suddenly I felt the rope tighten behind me and again I dropped on my axe. This time it was James, the lightest of all of us, who had gone in waste deep. A bit of pulling soon had him out.

My brain was by now on red alert and we were proceeding

cautiously when I caught site of a guy, with full kit, walking towards us completely alone. I warned him of the three crevasses we had just fallen into but he merely shrugged his shoulders and said he would take a different route. It seemed a strange thing to do.

I don't think there is a link here, but I heard later that a few days after this Claude Rey, the President of the International Guides Association (IFMGA) had died falling through into a crevasse when walking alone lower down on the same glacier.

We finally reached the Jungfraujoch and descended by train to the Klein Scheidegg and had just settled in at the station terrace, when the storm finally started. Yet again we had timed things to perfection, and armed with a cup of milky tea in my hand I felt a deep sense of satisfaction. I remembered my vow from all those years before, to climb the Eiger, Monch and Jungfrau, something which I had now fulfilled.

Importantly we had done it in good style. We had worked well as a team, and our experience had seen us through in tricky conditions. The Jungfrau had been a complete Alpine experience. We had overcome initial uncertainty, crossed glaciers, climbed rock and steep snow and ice. We had abseiled, dealt with crevasses and poor snow conditions, and had raced an incoming storm. The views had been stunning. We had barely seen another soul all day, and had climbed within guidebook time. Most importantly we had been in control throughout. I couldn't imagine a more complete and satisfying day out in the Alps. The contrast with my Eiger climb 23 years before could not have been more marked.

JR summed it up rather nicely on the train down to Grindelwald:

'I think we're all rather pleased with ourselves aren't we?' He said smiling.

Later that afternoon we met up with Mark at the Grindelwald Grund railway station, JR having informed him of our success by SMS text message whilst he was using the washing machines in the North Wall campsite in Grindelwald. He had recovered from his altitude sickness.

'I felt better by the time I reached the Kleine Scheidegg,' he said philosophically. He had later gone for a long walk on the surrounding hills and had spotted a new challenge for us on the Schynige Platte plateau.

After a wet rest day in Grindelwald, James and I accepted Mark's gauntlet. It involved climbing a rock pinnacle he had seen during his walk and was approached by taking the oldest mountain railway in Europe. This in itself had caught James's imagination and he hoped to see an original steam locomotive. We had no guidebook and didn't even have a name for the pinnacle. JR was happy to go for a walk by himself through the valley.

James was not disappointed as he saw an original working 19th century steam engine, and we relaxed as it took a long time to reach the plateau. Here we caught sight of Mark's objective, which looked both steep and loose. It was, and we carefully climbed the couple of pitches of grade III before we reached the summit. A rusty summit box suggested we were the first to come this way in two years, and it listed only a handful of ascents in the past thirty years.

Everything was loose and dangerous and we dislodged a large chunk of rock, but it was a fun interlude, completely unscripted and with a classic view of the North Walls of the Eiger, Mönch, and Jungfrau.

On our return we met up with Richard, Ana-Maria and their young sons Alexander and Andreas. Richard had been given leave of absence for a few days and wanted to climb the Finsteraarhorn (4274m). Mark and JR were keen to join him, which made me feel better because I had decided not to accompany them.

There were a number of reasons for this. A lack of sleep, combined with the fact that I had now climbed eight peaks in the past ten days, had left me feeling exhausted. Nor, deep down, did I relish taking on the extra risk. The images of Katie flashing before my eyes had been their own warning. The Finsteraarhorn, though certainly a magnificent challenge, would involve three more, hard, dangerous days, in scenery, which for a large part I had already just experienced.

I was quite happy to go off for a few days and find

something easy to solo, but then James decided not to do the Finsteraarhorn either and joined me. This was after I had suggested doing a long rock route, something he enjoys. We decided to go to Chamonix.

It was a relaxing, though not particularly successful, period in terms of summits. We crossed the Mer de Glace on our way to the Couvercle Hut, where we intended to climb the Aiguille du Moine (3412m) but on the vertical exposed ladders below the hut, I felt my arms cramping and decided to return. James was very good about it. After that, we did some rock climbing at the Rochers crag. Our proposed attempt on the Aiguille L'Index was cancelled because of another massive storm.

During this period we waited for news from the Oberland and were relieved to hear the others had climbed the Finsteraarhorn and were now safely back in the valley.

We had again witnessed a good deal of melting on the Mer de Glace and both James and I were amazed to compare both the current day states of the Boissons glacier and the Mer de Glace with the 19th century paintings which hung in the municipality museum in Chamonix.

We know a lot of this change will not be reversible, at least in our lifetimes. We also know that change in the Alps is to a certain extent a natural ongoing process. But the speed of this change seems to have increased recently and if we are to prevent things from getting a whole lot worse for our children and grandchildren we need serious action now. Fortunately, there is evidence that this message is beginning to receive more than just lip service from politicians, governments and business leaders right around the world.

During my last day in Chamonix I spent a long time thinking about the past quarter of a century. I had, by now, completed my 50th major Alpine ascent. Thirty-six of these involved 4000m peaks, although about a third of these were repeats. This was, therefore, little more than a quarter of the present 4000m list. How many more was I justified in trying to add? This is still the dilemma I have to wrestle with today. JR had identified part of the problem earlier in the trip. "We simply don't climb enough any more. We don't have time to spend weekend's away rock climbing and honing our skills and techniques."

I was no longer comfortable accepting the risks I had in the past. Not only was I incapable of the kind of technical climbing I had once done, but also I could not countenance random 'objective' danger in the way I had. I knew that my sub-conscious had been trying to tell me this for some time.

Another factor was reinforcing this view. Alpinism was becoming more dangerous. This was not just the conclusion of my own experiences, but was also being borne out by other reports. Those few weeks in July 2007, when we were climbing in the Alps, saw the worst accident rate amongst Alpinists ever.

On a our return, Mark sent us a report which described 2007 as one of the darkest summers of the last half century and stated that only in 1997 had so many climbers lost their lives, in such as short period of time. Bruno Jelk, chief of the Zermatt rescue services, stated that not only were more people going into the mountains without proper equipment, but that also these same mountains were becoming less stable every year due to the changing climate.

The report listed a long catalogue of deaths and accidents, many on routes we knew well, including the Barre des Ecrins where new serac falls had occurred.

At the same time Alpine guidebooks are being rewritten only a decade or so after they were first published, as long lists of amendments and notes are added about routes that are no longer the same or - in some cases - don't even exist anymore.

Alpinism is certainly a dangerous activity and I've had my fair share of luck over the years. I think an understanding of your limits is a crucial factor in staying alive and I would echo Nick Martin's words 'If I were to die in the mountains I'd be really, really pissed off.'

As I walked around Chamonix in the rain, I also considered the tremendous friendship and comradeship I have enjoyed over these years. Trusting others with your life and sharing hardships creates the same kind of bond that the military talk about, but in our case the conditions that have created it are more voluntary. These are friendships, which will last a lifetime.

Yet despite my concerns I will not stop visiting the Alps. I simply love the challenges, the places, the people, the views, and the history, in short the whole experience. But as I get older I will also begin exploring the world below the snowline with its pine forests, meadows and wooden huts. And in this way I will continue to play 'the Alpine game'.

*"I really don't think we need to
go back for your spare pair of socks."*

Part two

List of Alpine ascents in chronological order

This list covers the author's climbs as described in the text. It includes all 4000m peaks as defined at the time in the 1991 Richard Goedeke guidebook and his subsequent 2003 revision. Also taken into account is Martin Moran's excellent new guide, written for the Alpine Club and published in 2007. In my opinion this is the most logical 4000m-peak list yet produced.

1984 Eiger W Face solo.
1987 Matterhorn NE Ridge attempt - reached just below Solvay Hut.
1988 Mont Blanc NW Ridge, Dome du Gouter, Aiguille du Gouter.
1989 Mettlehorn, Breithorn SW Flank, Monte Rosa Dufourspitze W Ridge, Matterhorn NE Ridge.
1990 Attempt Eiger W Face - reached 150m from summit, Kilimanjaro Uhuru Peak & Gilmans Point, Mount Kenya Pt. Lenana.
1993 Lagginhorn SW ridge, Alphubel E Flank.
1994 Cima Piccolo SW Face to within one pitch of summit, Torre Grande, Breithorn SW flank, Castor NW flank, Allalinhorn NW Ridge.
1995 Mönch SE Ridge, Weismiess NW flank, Lagginhorn SW Ridge.
1996 Monte Rosa Vincent Pyramide, Corno Nero, Balmenhorn, Signalkuppe, Zumsteinspitze, Parrotspitze, Ludwigshowe, Midi-Plan Traverse, Petit Aiguille Verte.
1997 Gran Paradiso W flank, Mont Blanc de Tacul NW Face, Tour Ronde attempt, Breithorn SW Flank, Stockhorn.
1998 Breithorn SW Flank.
1999 Mirador, Tiraja, Huayna Potosi, Chacaltaya.
2000 Cristallino d'Ampezzo, Mittaghorn, Allalinhorn.
2001 Sugar Loaf Mountain, Bishorn NW Flank (long weekend).
2002 Breithorn SW Flank (long weekend).
2003 Breithorn SW Flank solo.
2004 Breithorn W & Central summits SW Flank (long weekend).

2005 Kilimanjaro Uhuru Peak & Gilmans point. Dome de Neige des Ecrins NE Face, Castor SE Ridge, Felixhorn SE Ridge, Allalinhorn NW Ridge, Cosmique Arête - Aiguille du Midi.
2006 Mt Kenya Pt. Lenana.
2007 Hohtali, Rote Nase, Stockhorn, Breithorn SW Flank, Riffelhorn, Oberothorn, Mönch SE Ridge, Jungfrau SE Ridge, 'Featchiehorn'.

Guide books we used over the years

Bernese Alps East, Robin G Collomb 1979, Alpine Club
Pennine Alps Central, Robin Collomb 1968 Alpine Club
Via Ferrata, Hofler Werner, 1992
Dolomites, Ron James, Alpine Club, 1988
Ecrins Massief, John Brailsford, Alpine club, 2002
The Alpine 4000m Peaks, Richard Goedeke 1991
The Alpine 4000m Peaks, Richard Goedeke, 2003
The 4000m Peaks of the Alps, Martin Moran, Alpine Club 2007

Explanation of climbing grades

There will always be an element of subjectivity about climbing grades. What constitutes a 'hard v diff' for one person might seem a 'severe' to someone else and, because each climb is different, it has to be judged separately. Also, the current conditions matter a great deal in the Alps. There is a big difference to doing a route in perfect dry conditions and doing it when it is covered in snow or ice. Nor will you be surprised to learn that the UK has its own way of rating rock climbs, which differs from the International standards.

Climbing grades.

Below is the formal UIAA rock climbing scale, along with the UK equivalent. My thoughts are also attached. (Please note these are my own subjective thoughts only and should not be seen as official statements.)

UIAA scale

I = Easy simple scrambling. If you are not a climber, or into climbing, this already seems like rock climbing. *If you suffer from vertigo even this level is probably not for you. With big boots on at altitude it is fun.*

II = Moderate/Difficult. By now even ordinary climbers think they are rock climbing properly. *Without rock boots and certainly in the wet, this is already a challenge to the ordinary climber. With plastic boots on, and at around 4000m this is a big challenge.*

III = Very Difficult. By now you are certainly rock climbing. *A good fun level for the ordinary climber – not too testing but still requiring thought and care. At altitude with plastic boots it is very tricky proposition.*

IV = Severe/Hard Severe (UK 4a, 4b) *A good challenge with rock boots on in the sun. At altitude with big boots it would be extremely hard for an ordinary climber.*

V = Very Severe/Hard Very Severe (UK 4c, 5a) *This was the hardest level I ever lead, when I was young and fit, and I cannot imagine doing it in big boots, let alone high altitude!*

VI = Hard Very Severe/Extremely Severe (UK 5a, 5b) *This is just the start of the real hard grades which still get pushed up a notch or two every now and then. There are not too many people climbing above this level. I managed some of this once at the Mile End climbing wall after months of practise!*

Alpine climbing grades

F – Facile. Simple glacier expeditions or snow ascents up to 40 degrees where the rope must be used; easy rock scrambles. This grade is the easiest one there is and if you don't like this you know that Alpinism is not for you.

PD – Peu Difficile. Crevassed or steeper glacier

expeditions; short exposed snow slopes up to 45-50 degrees. Narrow ridge crests, long rock scrambles, and shorter rock routes with pitches up to II/II+. This grade is where things get more serious. From experience there is a big difference between a PD- and a PD+ as one can seem very mild and easy whilst the other can make you feel life threatened. In general though this is a fun grade with enough challenges to keep you occupied.

AD – Assez Difficile. This involves snow and ice ascents with angles up to 55 degrees often requiring belays. Sustained narrow snow arêtes requiring good balance and crampon technique. Complex rock ridges with pitches up to III/III+ and occasional moves of IV, where abseils may be required. This covers routes like the Matterhorn and the Eiger normal routes and, for most ordinary climbers who are climbing unguided, this is quite stretching and probably as far as it goes. Above this things can get very scary.

D – Difficile. Steep face climbs on snow and ice up to 60 degrees. Seriously exposed and delicate snow ridges of considerable length. Major rock or mixed ridge climbs featuring rock pitches up to IV+ with short sections of V. This is scary but still imaginable, as at ground level back home in the sun with your rock boots on you will probably have a lot of experience of this level of rock climbing.

TD – Tres Difficile. Long snow and ice routes with complex route finding and pitches up to 75 degrees. Rock or mixed faces with sustained difficulties of IV, V and occasionally VI. You know this can be done because you have seen it on sun-drenched crags back home, but the thought of you - the ordinary climber - doing a route of this grade on a high altitude Alpine peak is preposterous.

ED – Extremement Difficile. Major face or couloir climbs. Sustained rock face and buttress routes with many pitches of V and VI. These are the kind of extreme climbs you read about in books or climbing magazines. As an ordinary climber this grade is best left to your dreams.

Above, sketch of the Breithorn in the morning sun.

Below, sketch of the view from the Mönch Hut.

Sketch of Team ID at the Gniffetti hut.

Summit of Mt Blanc du Tacul

Campsite Chamonix

View from summit of Gran Paradiso

Resting in Cham campsite

View from Vittorio Emanuel Hut

The Breithorn seen from the Stockhorn

The Players in 2007

Tony O'Flaherty   Richard Furlong   John Rothery (JR)

Nickolas Kelso   James Hunt   Mark Philips

Jeremy Baum   Will Kelso   Terrance Truscott

Acknowledgements

In writing this book I have reminded myself of the tremendous friendship and companionship I have enjoyed from a large number of people over the years, many of who are mentioned in this book. Special thanks should also go to James Hunt for his encouragement and many valuable suggestions during the months of writing. He is also responsible for the sketches, cartoons and maps in this book.

I would also like to thank Mark Phillips and Roger Sexton for their suggestions and help, which they volunteered so generously.

Finally, I would like to thank my family, who have endured my many Alpine adventures over the years without protest.

.